*Jeanette Valentine*
*Judith A. De Jong*
*Nancy J. Kennedy*
*Editors*

# Substance Abuse Prevention in Multicultural Communities

*Substance Abuse Prevention in Multicultural Communities* has been co-published simultaneously as *Drugs & Society*, Volume 12, Numbers 1/2 1998.

*Pre-publication REVIEWS, COMMENTARIES, EVALUATIONS . . .*

"**P**revention research has received increased attention in recent years with major review projects launched by both the Institute of Medicine and the National Institute on Mental Health. Research and practice has come to recognize that preventing problems and promoting positive development is healthier and more cost effective than treatment. This perspective, however, requires an unusual sensitivity to contextual factors relating to culture and ethnicity and to community characteristics.

*Substance Abuse Prevention in Multicultural Communities* makes a critically important contribution to the field by attending to each of these two sets of contextual variables. The volume's presentation of the historical evolution of prevention efforts as they have become increasingly community-based and sensitive to the different needs of ethnic groups

The Haworth Press, Inc.

# Substance Abuse Prevention in Multicultural Communities

*Substance Abuse Prevention in Multicultural Communities* has been co-published simultaneously as *Drugs & Society*, Volume 12, Numbers 1/2 1998.

The *Drugs & Society* Monographs/"Separates"

*Perspectives on Drug Use in the United States,* edited by Bernard Segal

*Moderation as a Goal or Outcome of Treatment for Alcohol Problems: A Dialogue,* edited by Mark B. Sobell and Linda C. Sobell

*Drug Use and Psychological Theory,* edited by S. W. Sadava

*Perspectives on Person-Environment Interaction and Drug-Taking Behavior,* edited by Bernard Segal

*Research Strategies in Alcoholism Treatment,* edited by Dan J. Lettieri

*Alcoholism Etiology and Treatment: Issues for Theory and Practice,* edited by Bernard Segal

*Perspectives on Adolescent Drug Use,* edited by Bernard Segal

*Current Issues in Alcohol/Drug Studies,* edited by Edith S. Lisansky Gomberg

*Drug-Taking Behavior Among School-Aged Youth: The Alaska Experience and Comparisons with Lower-48 States,* edited by Bernard Segal

*Addictive Disorders in Arctic Climates: Theory, Research, and Practice at the Novosibirsk Institute,* edited by Bernard Segal and Caesar P. Korolenko

*AIDS and Alcohol/Drug Abuse: Psychosocial Research,* edited by Dennis G. Fisher

*Homelessness and Drinking: A Study of a Street Population,* edited by Bernard Segal

*Ethnic and Multicultural Drug Abuse: Perspectives on Current Research,* edited by Joseph E. Trimble, Catherine S. Bolek, and Steve J. Niemcryk

*Drug Use in Rural American Communities,* edited by Ruth W. Edwards

*AIDS and Community-Based Drug Intervention Programs: Evaluation and Outreach,* edited by Dennis G. Fisher and Richard Needle

*Innovations in Alcoholism Treatment: State of the Art Reviews and Their Implications for Clinical Practice,* edited by Gerard J. Connors

*Prevention Practice in Substance Abuse,* edited by Carl G. Leukefeld and Richard R. Clayton

*Multicultural AIDS Prevention Programs,* edited by Robert T. Trotter II

*Sociocultural Perspectives on Volatile Solvent Use,* edited by Fred Beauvais and Joseph E. Trimble

*Substance Abuse Prevention in Multicultural Communities,* edited by Jeanette Valentine, Judith A. De Jong, and Nancy J. Kennedy

These books were published simultaneously as special thematic issues of *Drugs & Society* and are available bound separately. Visit Haworth's website at http://www.haworth.com to search our online catalog for complete tables of contents and ordering information for these and other publications. Or call 1-800-HAWORTH (outside US/Canada: 607-722-5857), Fax 1-800-895-0582 (outside US/Canada: 607-771-0012) or e-mail getinfo@haworth.com

# Substance Abuse Prevention in Multicultural Communities

Jeanette Valentine, PhD
Judith A. De Jong, PhD
Nancy J. Kennedy, DrPH
Editors

*Substance Abuse Prevention in Multicultural Communities* has been co-published simultaneously as *Drugs & Society*, Volume 12, Numbers 1/2 1998.

The Haworth Press, Inc.
New York • London

*Substance Abuse Prevention in Multicultural Communities* has been co-published simultaneously as *Drugs & Society*, Volume 12, Numbers 1/2 1998.

The Haworth Press, Inc., 10 Alice Street, Binghamton, NY 13904-1580 USA

Cover design by Thomas J. Mayshock Jr.

**Library of Congress Cataloging-in-Publication Data**

Substance abuse prevention in multicultural communities / Jeanette Valentine, Judith A. De Jong, Nancy J. Kennedy, editors.

    p. cm.

    "Has also been published as Drugs & society, volume 12, numbers 1/2, 1998"–T.p. verso.

    Includes bibliographical references and index.

    ISBN 0-7890-0343-0 (alk. paper)

    1. Substance abuse–United States–Prevention–Case studies. 2. Children of minorities–Substance use–United States. 3. Minorities–Substance use–United States. I. Valentine, Jeanette. II. De Jong, Judith Ann. III. Kennedy, Nancy J. (Nancy Jean), 1952-    .

    HV4999.2.S8 1998

    362.29'17'0973–dc21

                                                                  97-36612

                                                                   CIP

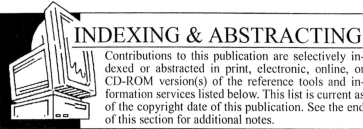

# INDEXING & ABSTRACTING

Contributions to this publication are selectively indexed or abstracted in print, electronic, online, or CD-ROM version(s) of the reference tools and information services listed below. This list is current as of the copyright date of this publication. See the end of this section for additional notes.

- *Abstracts in Anthropology,* Baywood Publishing Company, 26 Austin Avenue, P.O. Box 337, Amityville, NY 11701

- *Academic Abstracts/CD-ROM,* EBSCO Publishing Editorial Department, P.O. Box 590, Ipswich, MA 01938-0590

- *ADDICTION ABSTRACTS,* National Addiction Centre, 4 Windsor Walk, London SE5 8AF, England

- *ALCONLINE Database,* Centralforbundet for Alkohol-och narkotikaupplysning, Box 70412, 107 25 Stockholm, Sweden

- *Applied Social Sciences Index & Abstracts (ASSIA) (Online: ASSI via Data-Star) (CDRom: ASSIA Plus),* Bowker-Saur Limited, Maypole House, Maypole Road, East Grinstead, West Sussex, RH19 1HH, England

- *Brown University Digest of Addiction Theory and Application, The (DATA Newsletter),* Project Cork Institute, Dartmouth Medical School, 14 South Main Street, Suite 2F, Hanover, NH 03755-2015

- *Cambridge Scientific Abstracts, Health & Safety Science Abstracts,* 7200 Wisconsin Avenue #601, Bethesda, MD 20814

- *Child Development Abstracts & Bibliography,* University of Kansas, 213 Bailey Hall, Lawrence, KS 66045

- *CNPIEC Reference Guide: Chinese National Directory of Foreign Periodicals,* P.O. Box 88, Beijing, People's Republic of China

- *Criminal Justice Abstracts,* Willow Tree Press, 15 Washington Street, 4th Floor, Newark, NJ 07102

- *Criminal Justice Periodical Index,* University Microfilms, Inc., P. O. Box 32770, Louisville, KY 40232

(continued)

- *Excerpta Medica/Secondary Publishing Division,* Elsevier Science, Inc., Secondary Publishing Division, 655 Avenue of the Americas, New York, NY 10010

- *Family Studies Database (online and CD/ROM),* National Information Services Corporation, 306 East Baltimore Pike, 2nd Floor, Media, PA 19063

- *Health Source: Indexing & Abstracting of 160 selected health related journals, updated monthly:* EBSCO Publishing, 83 Pine Street, Peabody, MA 01960

- *Health Source Plus: expanded version of "Health Source" to be released shortly:* EBSCO Publishing, 83 Pine Street, Peabody, MA 01960

- *Human Resources Abstracts (HRA),* Sage Publications, Inc., 2455 Teller Road, Newbury Park, CA 91320

- *IBZ International Bibliography of Periodical Literature,* Zeller Verlag GmbH & Co., P.O.B. 1949, d-49009 Osnabruck, Germany

- *Index to Periodical Articles Related to Law,* University of Texas, 727 East 26th Street, Austin, TX 78705

- *International Pharmaceutical Abstracts,* ASHP, 7272 Wisconsin Avenue, Bethesda, MD 20814

- *International Political Science Abstracts,* 27 Rue Saint-Guillaume, F-75337 Paris, Cedex 07, France

- *INTERNET ACCESS (& additional networks) Bulletin Board for Libraries ("BUBL") coverage of information resources on INTERNET, JANET, and other networks.*
  - <URL:http://bubl.ac.uk/>
  - The new locations will be found under <URL:http://bubl.ac.uk/link/>.
  - Any existing BUBL users who have problems finding information on the new service should contact the BUBL help line by sending e-mail to <bubl@bubl.ac.uk>.
  The Andersonian Library, Curran Building, 101 St. James Road, Glasgow G4 0NS, Scotland

- *Medication Use STudies (MUST) DATABASE,* The University of Mississippi, School of Pharmacy, University, MS 38677

(continued)

- *Mental Health Abstracts (online through DIALOG),* IFI/Plenum Data Company, 3202 Kirkwood Highway, Wilmington, DE 19808

- *NIAAA Alcohol and Alcohol Problems Science Database (ETOH),* National Institute on Alcohol Abuse and Alcoholism, 1400 Eye Street NW, Suite 600, Washington, DC 20005

- *Personnel Management Abstracts,* 704 Island Lake Road, Chelsea, MI 48118

- *Psychological Abstracts (PsycINFO),* American Psychological Association, P.O. Box 91600, Washington, DC 20090-1600

- *Public Affairs Information Bulletin (PAIS),* Public Affairs Information Service, Inc., 521 West 43rd Street, New York, NY 10036-4396

- *Referativnyi Zhurnal (Abstracts Journal of the Institute of Scientific Information of the Republic of Russia),* The Institute of Scientific Information, Baltijskaja ul., 14, Moscow A-219, Republic of Russia

- *Sage Family Studies Abstracts (SFSA),* Sage Publications, Inc., 2455 Teller Road, Newbury Park, CA 91320

- *Social Planning/Policy & Development Abstracts (SOPODA),* Sociological Abstracts, Inc., P.O. Box 22206, San Diego, CA 92192-0206

- *Social Work Abstracts,* National Association of Social Workers, 750 First Street NW, 8th Floor, Washington, DC 20002

- *Sociological Abstracts (SA),* Sociological Abstracts, Inc., P.O. Box 22206, San Diego, CA 92192-0206

- *SOMED (social medicine) Database,* Landes Institut fur Den Offentlichen Gesundheitsdienst NRW, Postfach 20 10 12, D-33548 Bielefeld, Germany

- *Sport Search,* Sport Information Resource Centre, 1600 James Naismith Drive, Suite 107, Gloucester, Ontario K1B 5N4, Canada

- *Violence and Abuse Abstracts: A Review of Current Literature on Interpersonal Violence (VAA),* Sage Publications, Inc., 2455 Teller Road, Newbury Park, CA 91320

(continued)

# SPECIAL BIBLIOGRAPHIC NOTES

*related to special journal issues (separates)*
*and indexing/abstracting*

- ❏ indexing/abstracting services in this list will also cover material in any "separate" that is co-published simultaneously with Haworth's special thematic journal issue or DocuSerial. Indexing/abstracting usually covers material at the article/chapter level.

- ❏ monographic co-editions are intended for either non-subscribers or libraries which intend to purchase a second copy for their circulating collections.

- ❏ monographic co-editions are reported to all jobbers/wholesalers/approval plans. The source journal is listed as the "series" to assist the prevention of duplicate purchasing in the same manner utilized for books-in-series.

- ❏ to facilitate user/access services all indexing/abstracting services are encouraged to utilize the co-indexing entry note indicated at the bottom of the first page of each article/chapter/contribution.

- ❏ this is intended to assist a library user of any reference tool (whether print, electronic, online, or CD-ROM) to locate the monographic version if the library has purchased this version but not a subscription to the source journal.

- ❏ individual articles/chapters in any Haworth publication are also available through the Haworth Document Delivery Service (HDDS).

# Substance Abuse Prevention in Multicultural Communities

## CONTENTS

# ABOUT THE EDITORS

**Jeanette Valentine, PhD,** is a Research Specialist at the Children's Hospital and Medical Center of Seattle, Washington. The work for this volume was carried out when Dr. Valentine directed the New England Health and Poverty Action Center, a program of the Division of General Pediatrics, Department of Pediatrics, of the Floating Hospital and Tufts University School of Medicine. Dr. Valentine has evaluated numerous adolescent health intervention programs, including teen pregnancy prevention and care, school-based clinics, adolescent health promotion, interpersonal violence, and substance abuse prevention.

**Judith A. De Jong, PhD,** has 20 years of professional experience in research, beginning with studies of the social development of children and progressing to work related to addictions and the prevention of substance abuse. During the course of the Center for Substance Abuse Prevention (CSAP) demonstration programs described in this volume, Dr. De Jong was the Federal Project Officer providing oversight to a group of primarily Native American High-Risk Youth Prevention demonstration programs, as well as directing the development of CSAP's Second Cross-Site Evaluation.

**Nancy J. Kennedy, DrPH,** has 25 years of professional and personal experience in the fields of mental health and substance abuse. She is currently the Director of Managed Care for the Center for Substance Abuse Prevention (CSAP) and is the prevention liaison to the managed care initiative under the auspices of the Substance Abuse and Mental Health Services Administration (SAMHSA). Prior to CSAP, she worked as an epidemiologist at the National Institute on Drug Abuse.

# Preface

The substance abuse prevention field is a relatively new discipline in spite of the longevity of the problem of alcohol and drugs throughout the history of this country. As the former Director of the Center for Substance Abuse Prevention (CSAP), the lead Federal agency for the prevention of substance abuse, I had the pleasure of seeing the creation and development of hundreds of different demonstration prevention projects throughout the country. A wealth of information has emanated from these demonstrations targeted to culturally diverse populations.

One such demonstration program that CSAP designed targeted youth with an increased statistical probability of drug use leading to substance abuse and possible addictive disease. In contrast to a standard research protocol, demonstrations can document and measure effects of multiple interventions which more commonly exemplify the complexity associated with drug-taking behavior. Several of these CSAP programs, referred to as high risk youth demonstrations, are chronicled in this volume.

The variety of innovative, community-based programs designed to increase knowledge of effective substance abuse prevention strategies for the high risk youth population utilized the logic model developed by CSAP staff. The logic model is a conceptual framework that links, analytically, (a) the problems or factors that are considered to have an impact on the incidence of substance abuse; (b) the proposed project's strategies to reduce specific risk factors and/or enhance specific protective factors; (c) the plan to implement the strategies; and (d) the anticipated outcomes.

These articles illustrate various aspects of the logic model. Some authors focus on the design and implementation phases of the model, while other authors explicate the selection of strategies relative to the correlates

---

The contents of this preface are the sole responsibility of the author and do not necessarily represent the official views of the funding agency.

[Haworth co-indexing entry note]: "Preface." Johnson, Elaine M. Co-published simultaneously in *Drugs & Society* (The Haworth Press, Inc.) Vol. 12, No. 1/2, 1998, pp. xiii-xiv; and: *Substance Abuse Prevention in Multicultural Communities* (ed: Jeanette Valentine, Judith A. De Jong, and Nancy J. Kennedy) The Haworth Press, Inc., 1998, pp. xiii-xiv. Single or multiple copies of this article are available for a fee from The Haworth Document Delivery Service [1-800-342-9678, 9:00 a.m. - 5:00 p.m. (EST). E-mail address: getinfo@haworth.com].

or risk factors, for substance abuse found in any of the following domains: the individual, the family, the school, the peer group, the work place, and the neighborhood or community. The authors of the remaining articles focus on the outcome findings from the demonstration programs.

These papers were invited, subjected to peer review and edited by Dr. Jeanette Valentine, an experienced researcher who conducted CSAP program evaluations, Dr. Judith De Jong, a former project officer associated with the high risk youth cross-site evaluation effort, and Dr. Nancy Kennedy, a senior staff member of CSAP. I wish to thank them, as well as the authors of the papers included in this volume, for their work and dedication.

Finally, it is critical that we all continue to assist in the maturation and collegiality of the prevention field so as to determine why many people, especially youth, are drawn to drug use and why some succumb to addictive diseases.

*Elaine M. Johnson, PhD*
*Former Director*
*Office/Center for Substance*
*Abuse Prevention*
*Professor*
*Morgan State University*
*Department of Social Work*
*Baltimore, MD*

# Implementation and Evaluation of Substance Abuse Prevention Programs in Culturally Diverse Communities: An Introduction

Judith A. De Jong, PhD
Jeanette Valentine, PhD
Nancy J. Kennedy, DrPH

"I feel that I can talk to my father." The year was 1990; the place, a meeting of evaluators working with prevention programs in Asian American communities. This standard item from a family environment scale had been proffered by a federal project officer as an example of an item which could be used to measure outcomes in a standardized cross-site questionnaire. An evaluator responded that in his culture, it was not appropriate that a son discuss things with his father. He explained that when the topic was not something which could be handled through discussions with the mother, the uncle was the appropriate person to consult. The discussion

Judith A. De Jong is currently an independent consultant acting as a grant writer and evaluator on adolescent prevention programs, Lanham, MD. Jeanette Valentine is Research Specialist at the Children's Hospital and Medical Center, Seattle, WA. Nancy J. Kennedy is Director of Managed Care for the Center for Substance Abuse Prevention (CSAP) and is the Prevention Liaison to the managed care initiative under the auspices of the Substance Abuse and Mental Health Service Administration (SAMHSA).

The contents of this article are the sole responsibility of the authors and do not necessarily represent the official views of the funding agency.

[Haworth co-indexing entry note]: "Implementation and Evaluation of Substance Abuse Prevention Programs in Culturally Diverse Communities: An Introduction." De Jong, Judith A., Jeanette Valentine, and Nancy J. Kennedy. Co-published simultaneously in *Drugs & Society* (The Haworth Press, Inc.) Vol. 12, No. 1/2, 1998, pp. 1-5; and: *Substance Abuse Prevention in Multicultural Communities* (ed: Jeanette Valentine, Judith A. De Jong, and Nancy J. Kennedy) The Haworth Press, Inc., 1998, pp. 1-5. Single or multiple copies of this article are available for a fee from The Haworth Document Delivery Service [1-800-342-9678, 9:00 a.m. - 5:00 p.m. (EST). E-mail address: getinfo@haworth.com].

*1*

broadened into questions of how to determine desirability of specific outcomes in a population undergoing acculturation. This interchange illustrates only one of the complex issues faced by demonstration prevention programs funded by the Center for Substance Abuse Prevention (CSAP) in developing and evaluating substance abuse prevention programs in minority communities.

In the past decade, concern over drug and alcohol abuse among children and adolescents has led to funding of research into the etiology and prevention of substance abuse. Approaches to prevention have multiplied, reflecting a range of theories. These attribute the problem variously to individual factors (genetic, emotional, knowledge, attitude, etc.) and environmental factors in the family, school, peer group, community, economic system and society at large (Hawkins, Catalano & Miller 1992; De Jong, 1995). In 1987, the Office for Substance Abuse Prevention (OSAP, later CSAP), funded 130 demonstration programs for the prevention of substance abuse among high risk youth. The first of the articles in this issue describes one of these first generation projects, Friendly PEERsuasion[SM]. This program implemented and rigorously evaluated a configuration of individually-focused interventions for African American, female adolescents. The program faced a number of the challenges to research methodology described by Moskowitz (1993), including small sample size and problems with fidelity of intervention implementation at replication sites. Despite these limitations, the program produced some intriguing preliminary results indicating the importance of developmental timing of interventions.

In the decade following this first generation of programs, a second generation of programs was funded by OSAP/CSAP. This second generation was encouraged to design more comprehensive prevention programs, focusing on multiple risk factors for substance abuse (Goplerud, 1990), and was confronted with increasingly greater demands for process and outcome evaluation. The majority of these programs were funded in minority communities in which the etiology of the problem had received little attention from researchers. As a consequence of these funding parameters, program designers were faced with designing programs for populations on which there was scanty data with regard to epidemiology, but of whom it was known there existed a plethora of those factors found to be associated with risk for substance abuse in the general population. Program evaluators were faced, not only with the difficulties that Moskowitz (1993) documents in his review of design problems in prevention research, but additional problems such as: lack of instruments calibrated for minority populations, high mobility of inner city urban populations, and a

suspicion of researchers based on past exploitation of minority populations in research studies. A more advanced approach to design of interventions and the study of these interventions evolved. The characteristics of
this second generation of intervention programs are illustrated by the
remaining eight articles in this issue.

A defining characteristic of the second generation was the customiza-
tion of interventions. The first generation of OSAP/CSAP programs had
generally experimented with limited interventions, documenting participation and satisfaction (services evaluation), and testing effects of a specific
protocol. What became clear from the information provided by this first
generation of programs was that the effects of multiple risk factors often
overwhelmed the impact of single interventions and that local characteristics and input needed to be taken into account in customizing and implementing programs. The second generation of OSAP/CSAP programs was,
therefore, asked to change its focus to a demonstration logic model (Bass,
1991), one which defined the sources or correlates of the problem in a
specific population, and selected multiple interventions which would stra-
tegically address multiple contributors to the problem. In this approach,
program development emerged out of a dialectic between theory and
grassroots input. Three of the articles, those by Laquer, McDonald and
Sayger, and Van Stelle et al. focus on this aspect of the demonstration
process. Laquer provides a detailed description of how the Nee-kon project used theory and local knowledge to address multiple precursors of
school failure in young Native American children. McDonald and Sayger
describe the FAST program, one solidly based both in theory and practical
research which uses a simple but multifaceted strategy to simultaneously
build intra- and extra-familial social support structures. Van Stelle et al.
describe an extensive wraparound program.

The second generation approach emphasized collaboration. Resources
of multiple agencies were tied together in joint collaborative efforts.
Godley and Velasquez describe the Logan Square project, a coordinated
interagency effort which appears to have reduced gang involvement, a
major risk factor for later substance abuse for their inner city Latino
population.

The new demonstration programs encouraged innovative evolution,
rather than rigid adherence to specific protocols. Aktan details how, during
the course of her project, the intervention broadened in scope, the curriculum was extensively rewritten and the evaluation modified. Petoskey et al.
report on use of an open-ended community component to increase individual and communal empowerment.

The second generation application of multiple interventions to multiple domains (family, school, peer group, community, etc.), had a number of implications for evaluators. It made random assignment to conditions impossible in most programs, as self-selection would necessarily be operative in determining participation in at least some of the interventions. The implementation of multiple interventions required more investment per capita, both in interventions and in evaluation of those interventions. The number of subjects was, therefore, decreased, while the number of intervention conditions multiplied. Allowing innovation and community input to change interventions during the course of a project further complicated definition of protocol and criteria for quality control. Multifaceted interventions which included community and school components affected potential control groups within the community or school, while comparison groups from outside the systems could be questionable matches for the treatment population. Given these circumstances, evaluation was forced into a broader, more exploratory role. Outcome evaluation used quasi experimental strategies aimed at determining initial conditions and dosages received and relating them to general outcomes. These articles describe a variety of such designs. Godley and Velasquez use an institutional cycles quasi-experimental research design. Petoskey et al. combined a comparison group design using quantitative data for their school population and a case study approach to the larger context of community change. McDonald & Sayger and Valentine et al. work with selected, hard to match groups of youth who are already exhibiting problem behavior; their designs use comparison parameters based on normal and clinical populations to measure movement toward the norm. Dose-response modeling is used by Valentine et al., while comparisons between results of different amounts and types of dosages are used by Zane et al.

The programs described in this volume home in on the risk factors, or "barriers to healthy lifestyles" faced by children or adolescents at different developmental stages. The Nee-kon program worked with preschool children at risk for future school failure. Two programs, Safe Haven and FAST, were family programs, the former designed for parents in substance abuse treatment, the latter working with families of children already exhibiting problem behavior in school. Family Circles combined a family curriculum with revival of traditional Native American practices and community building. Logan Square focused on Latino children and adolescents who were being recruited for gang membership. The school-based program described by Zane et al. for Asian American youth at a similar age level, addresses social, family, cultural, and school problems which intensify during transitions to middle school and high school. Friendly PEERsuasion provided a strong life skills and substance abuse education program for African American, female adolescents at a stage where substance use was being initiated. The Red Cliff Wellness program was oriented by a strong spiritual and empowerment focus in both school and community curricula. Urban Youth Connection developed a counseling program designed to aid middle and high school Latino and African American adolescents in Boston.

As a group, these articles demonstrate the wide range of creativity and adaptability which is required of demonstration program staff and evaluators. To prevention professionals, these articles offer a wealth of experience on how to successfully design and implement prevention programs. Researchers will appreciate the collaboration achieved by these projects between evaluators and program staff, and the creative solutions they have developed.

## REFERENCES

Bass, R. (1991). The logic model for OSAP high risk grantees. Unpublished Manuscript, Division of Demonstrations for High Risk Populations, Center for Substance Abuse Prevention.

De Jong, J. (1995). An approach for high risk prevention research. *Drugs & Society,* 8, 125-138.

Goplerud, E. ed. (1990). Breaking new ground for youth at risk: program summaries. OSAP Technical Report 1, Office for Substance Abuse Prevention, Rockville, MD.

Hawkins, J.D., Catalano, R.F., and Miller, J.Y. (1992). Risk and protective factors for alcohol and other drug problems in adolescence and early adulthood: implications for substance abuse prevention. *Psych. Bull.,* 112, 1-41.

Moskowitz, J.M. (1993). Why reports of outcome evaluations are often biased or uninterpretable; examples from evaluations of drug abuse prevention programs. *Evaluation and Program Planning,* 16, 1-9.

# Friendly PEERsuasion[SM] Against Substance Use: The Girls Incorporated[SM] Model and Evaluation

Faedra Lazar Weiss, MAHL
Heather Johnston Nicholson, PhD

**SUMMARY.** Girls Incorporated Friendly PEERsuasion is a leadership and substance abuse prevention program based on the social influence model. Girls in grades 6-8 considered to be at high risk for substance use were recruited in four geographically and ethnically diverse communities, with participants randomly assigned to Fall 1988 "treatment" and Spring 1989 "comparison" participation

Faedra Lazar Weiss is Research Associate at the Girls Incorporated National Resource Center, 441 W. Michigan Street, Indianapolis, IN 46202-3287. Heather Johnston Nicholson is Director of the National Resource Center and Girls Incorporated Associate Executive Director for Research, Program and Training.

The authors would like to acknowledge the Center for Substance Abuse Prevention, which supported the implementation of Friendly PEERsuasion, and CSAP and the William T. Grant Foundation, which supported evaluation of this program; lead evaluator Marcia R. Chaiken, PhD of LINC and evaluators Michael D. Maltz, PhD, Christine Smith, MA, and Stephen D. Kennedy, PhD of Abt Associates; Project Director Dolores Wisdom; and the national and local staff of Girls Incorporated and the young women who made the evaluation possible. We also appreciate the assistance of Judith De Jong and Jeanette Valentine in preparing this article. The contents of this article are the sole responsibility of the authors and do not necessarily represent the official views of the funding agency.

[Haworth co-indexing entry note]: "Friendly PEERsuasion[SM] Against Substance Use: The Girls Incorporated[SM] Model and Evaluation." Weiss, Faedra Lazar, and Heather Johnston Nicholson. Co-published simultaneously in *Drugs & Society* (The Haworth Press, Inc.) Vol. 12, No. 1/2, 1998, pp. 7-22; and: *Substance Abuse Prevention in Multicultural Communities* (ed: Jeanette Valentine, Judith A. De Jong, and Nancy J. Kennedy) The Haworth Press, Inc., 1998, pp. 7-22. Single or multiple copies of this article are available for a fee from The Haworth Document Delivery Service [1-800-342-9678, 9:00 a.m. - 5:00 p.m. (EST). E-mail address: getinfo@haworth.com].

7

(delayed entry model). Outcomes of interest were avoiding any use of harmful substances and leaving situations in which peers were using harmful substances. At the Birmingham, Alabama program site, where the program was implemented almost exactly as designed, an evaluation using survival analysis techniques included 118 girls (47 treatment, 71 comparison). A second evaluation using logistic regression compared the behavior of 354 participants (152 treatment, 202 comparison) across all four sites. Friendly PEERsuasion proved moderately effective, particularly for the youngest participants ($p < .10$). Evaluation results and subsequent research suggest that most girls experiment with substance use in their early teens and that the preteen years are a critical time for intervention. *[Article copies available for a fee from The Haworth Document Delivery Service: 1-800-342-9678. E-mail address: getinfo@haworth.com]*

## INTRODUCTION AND BACKGROUND

In 1988-1989 Girls Incorporated (formerly Girls Clubs of America) expanded its comprehensive health and sexuality programming with the introduction of Friendly PEERsuasion. This program, based on the social influence model, was designed to help girls ages 11 through 14 acquire knowledge, skills and support systems to avoid substance abuse. This article describes the program design, implementation in four Girls Incorporated affiliates and evaluation of the program at these demonstration sites.

During the mid-1980s national attention to the health hazards and societal costs attributable to substance use led to sharply decreased tolerance for any use of illicit drugs or abuse of the licit drugs alcohol and tobacco. The percentage of young people reporting substance use, after rising throughout the 1970s, began to decline in the early 1980s (Elliott & Huizinga, 1984; Johnston, O'Malley, & Bachman, 1986) but remained at unacceptably high levels (Johnston et al., 1986). At the same time, several studies documented that young people involved in substance use beyond experimentation are often at risk in multiple areas of their lives (Elliott & Huizinga; Kandel, Simcha-Fagan, & Davies, 1985). Based on experience with teenage girls nationwide and the newly developing body of gender-specific research on substance abuse, Girls Incorporated took the lead in developing programming that takes into account the patterns, causes and consequences of substance abuse particular to girls.

Available research suggested some gender differences in the causes of substance abuse. Peer pressure to use substances may be more of a factor for girls than boys (Girls Clubs of America [Girls Incorporated], 1988).

Girls tend to use substances in groups and to use substances that can be purchased legally; when girls use illegal drugs, these are often supplied by boys as part of a dating or sexual relationship (Bodinger-de Uriarte & Austin, 1991). Girls disproportionately report using cigarettes and over-the-counter diet pills in their efforts to come closer to the almost impossible thinness that is currently considered attractive (Jackson, 1982; Johnston et al., 1986, 1995; National Center on Addiction and Substance Abuse [CASA], 1996).

In addition, where boys under stress tend to "act out," girls frequently turn to covert, often self-destructive behavior such as drug and alcohol abuse (Brunswick & Messeri, 1984; Girls Incorporated, 1996; Kandel, Simcha-Fagan, & Davies, 1985). For girls there is a strong link between substance abuse and sexual, emotional or physical abuse. Girls who have learned too well that it is not "ladylike" to act assertively even in self-preservation or who meet disbelief when they appeal to adults for help may resort to drugs to cover up the pain of stress and abuse rather than engage in outwardly directed action to stop the sources of pain. Girls with disabilities may be especially likely to use substances: to live with pain, to make loneliness or boredom more bearable, or to cope with ongoing dependence (Rousso, 1986). In sum, girls' substance abuse often reflects the combination of an untenable situation and the perception of powerlessness to change the situation or leave it (cf. Gilligan, 1982).

## INTERVENTION

*Evolution of Friendly PEERsuasion.* By the mid-1980s substance abuse prevention programs had already evolved through four stages: moral and legal objections to substance use, scare tactics, knowledge as deterrent, and generic esteem-building and decision-making skills (see Girls Clubs of America [Girls Incorporated], 1988). Evaluations of the fifth generation of programs, based on social influence and life skills models, suggested that prevention programs with a balance of adult and peer leadership might be particularly effective with girls (Perry & Murray, 1985; Tobler, 1986).

As a national organization committed to positive youth development, Girls Incorporated has helped young women grow up strong, smart and bold[SM] for over fifty years. With over a thousand program sites in 35 states, Girls Incorporated serves over 350,000 young people yearly, most of them girls and young women.

Girls Incorporated has always served a large number of girls and young women considered at high risk for substance abuse. Many of the organization's centers are located in neighborhoods where substance abuse is an acknowledged problem. In 1983 the national organization adopted a policy statement committing the organization "to helping girls acquire positive health habits, accurate information, decision-making skills and an attitude of personal responsibility for their own health" in four areas, one of which was substance abuse (Girls Clubs of America [Girls Incorporated], 1983). The national health promotion program Girl Power: Health Power (Girls Clubs of America [Girls Incorporated], 1985) included six sessions on substance abuse. Local Girls Incorporated affiliates overwhelmingly reported offering programming in health education to the girls and young women they served in 1984 (88%) and in substance abuse prevention in 1988 (also 88%).

*Goals.* In 1987 Girls Incorporated was awarded funding by the Center (formerly Office) for Substance Abuse Prevention to develop a gender-specific substance abuse prevention program. Friendly PEERsuasion grew out of two substance abuse prevention programs developed by Girls Incorporated affiliate Girls and Youth Services of Arlington (Texas): YAAA! (Youth Alcohol Awareness and Alternatives) Team and Winner's Circle. Both programs had earned positive evaluations and national program awards. A team of national and local Girls Incorporated staff and evaluation consultants integrated elements from both programs into a curriculum designed to prevent initial use of all types of substances and developed the surveys and forms used in program evaluation. This affiliate began to field-test draft versions of Friendly PEERsuasion curriculum and evaluation materials in October 1987 and continued to implement the program throughout the study period. However, data from Arlington participants was not included in the formal evaluations.

*Target population.* Friendly PEERsuasion draws upon the social influence and life skills models of prevention, using a combination of adult leadership and peer reinforcement to develop the skills, knowledge and support systems that girls need in order to identify and respond critically to messages and social pressures that encourage substance use. Girls of middle school age (generally ages 11-14) were identified as the primary target population for several reasons. First, many girls try drugs for the first time during their middle school years. Also, the prevention strategies used in Friendly PEERsuasion fit particularly well with the strengths and needs of this age group–making one's own decisions but with adult support and guidance; learning how to resist peer pressure without losing friends; finding adult role models, creating a positive peer group and becoming role models for younger children.

*Program activities.* In the first phase of the program, the girls participate in 14 hour-long sessions facilitated by a trained adult leader. Through hands-on, interactive and enjoyable activities such as games, group discussions and role plays, participants learn about the short-term and long-term effects of substance abuse, experience healthy ways to manage stress, learn to recognize media and peer pressure to use drugs, practice skills for making responsible decisions about licit and illicit drug use and prepare to become peer leaders. Each session focuses on a particular objective while reinforcing skills and knowledge introduced in previous sessions. After completing this core curriculum the participants are certified as PEERsuaders[SM].

In the second phase of the program, small teams of PEERsuaders[SM] plan and implement eight to ten half-hour sessions of substance abuse prevention activities for PEERsuade-Me's[SM] (children ages 6 through 10). Working with their adult leaders, PEERsuaders draw on the skills and activities introduced in the first phase of the program and their own experiences and creativity to present factual information and to model and practice skills, attitudes and behaviors related to substance abuse prevention.

*Site selection.* All Girls Incorporated affiliates were invited to apply as demonstration sites. Four organizations–Girls Incorporated of Central Alabama (Birmingham), Girls Incorporated of Pinellas County (Clearwater, Florida, then working with and now part of Girls Incorporated of Pinellas, Pinellas Park, Florida), Girls Incorporated of Rapid City (South Dakota) and Girls Incorporated of Worcester (Massachusetts)–were chosen on the basis of their high-quality program services, organizational capacity and service to young teens and children considered at high risk of early substance use. Care was taken to include affiliates serving girls of differing ethnic and racial backgrounds and living in a variety of high-risk situations. Beginning in June 1988 these sites also field-tested program and evaluation materials.

## EVALUATION STRATEGY–OVERVIEW

Each demonstration site was asked to recruit at least 100 girls between the ages of 11 and 14 to participate as PEERsuaders. To avoid the ethical problem of withholding a program that Girls Incorporated expected to be effective, the evaluation employed a delayed entry design. Approximately 40 percent of girls completing the preprogram survey were assigned randomly to fall participation in Friendly PEERsuasion, becoming the treatment group. The remaining girls became the comparison group, assigned to participate in Friendly PEERsuasion the following spring.

Study participants at all four sites were asked to complete four questionnaires. At the preprogram questionnaire (September 1988) neither group had participated in Friendly PEERsuasion; at the third postprogram questionnaire (May 1989) both groups had completed the program. Data from the two intermediate questionnaires provide the best approximation to experimental and control groups. At the first postprogram questionnaire (November 1988) the fall group had completed PEERsuader training and at the second postprogram questionnaire (February 1989) had also taught PEERsuade-Me's while the spring group had yet to participate in the program. Outcomes of interest, avoidance of substance use and leaving situations where peers were using substances, were measured through self-reports of participation in a variety of activities, including substance use. Three of the four questionnaires also collected background information related to high risk of substance use. Additional forms, completed by participants and adult leaders, collected information about individual levels of program participation.

## *EVALUATION PLAN–GIRLS INCORPORATED OF CENTRAL ALABAMA (Chaiken, Maltz & Smith, 1990)*

Girls Incorporated of Central Alabama offered Friendly PEERsuasion during school hours in two Birmingham public schools offering kindergarten through grade 8. Demographic characteristics of the community served by the schools suggested that students were at particularly high risk of substance use. However, these schools had not yet implemented any other prevention programs.

*Participant characteristics.* All girls in grades 6 through 8 attending the two schools at which Friendly PEERsuasion would be offered were invited to participate. Of the 127 girls completing the preprogram questionnaire, 49 were assigned to the fall "treatment" group and 78 to the spring "comparison" group. Demographic characteristics of the participants can be found in Table 1. Participants' responses on the preprogram questionnaire suggested that these girls were at high risk for substance abuse (Table 2).

*Program implementation.* In this close-to-ideal situation Friendly PEERsuasion was implemented almost exactly as designed. Because the program was offered during school time, all enrolled participants had to come to program sessions; the engaging activities convinced virtually every initially unenthusiastic participant to become involved. Average attendance in both fall and spring was 12 sessions. On a scale of 0 (very hostile) through 5 (bored) to 10 (very positive), program leaders' ratings of participants' attitudes averaged between 8 and 9, with no average ratings below 6.5. Almost all curriculum activities were completed; participants reported enjoying more than 90 percent of curriculum activities and

TABLE 1. Racial/Ethnic Background of Girls Participating in Friendly PEER-suasion[SM], Fall 1988-Spring 1989, by Girls Incorporated Affiliate

**Girls Incorporated affiliate**

| Race/ethnicity | Rapid City (n = 55) | Pinellas (n = 104) | Central Alabama (n = 127) | Worcester (n = 68) | all sites (n = 354) |
|---|---|---|---|---|---|
| African-American, non-Latina | 4% | 72% | 88% | 9% | 55% |
| European descent (nonminority) | 47% | 14% | 1% | 31% | 18% |
| Latina (may be of any race) | 6% | 5% | 8% | 49% | 14% |
| Native American (American Indian) | 44% | 7% | 2% | 7% | 11% |
| not reported | 0% | 2% | 1% | 4% | 2% |

**Not all percentages add to 100 due to rounding**
Source: preprogram questionnaires; Smith & Kennedy (1991), Table 1

learning something from more than 85 percent (girls did not always recognize they were learning while having fun).

*Evaluation methodology.* Differences in self-reported behaviors of the fall and spring program groups over the study period were compared using Pearson's *r.* Survival analyses were used to compare self-reported behaviors of girls by program group and also within and across program groups by age cohort. Almost all participants (93%) provided enough data to be included in the evaluation.

All participants were regarded as having a clean slate at the beginning of the intervention. Any subsequent substance use self-reported on any of the postprogram questionnaires, whether of alcohol, tobacco or drugs illegal for adults, was considered a failure. Similarly, a self-report on any postprogram questionnaire of failing to leave a situation in which peers were using licit or illicit substances was considered a failure on that variable.

## *EVALUATION FINDINGS–GIRLS INCORPORATED OF CENTRAL ALABAMA*

Questionnaire responses indicated that participants, particularly the younger participants (ages 11-12), were at a critical time in their lives for

TABLE 2. Factors Indicating High Risk of Substance Use for Girls Participating in Friendly PEERsuasion[SM], Fall 1988-Spring 1989, by Girls Incorporated Affiliate

| | Girls Incorporated affiliate | | | | |
|---|---|---|---|---|---|
| | Rapid City (n = 55) | Pinellas (n = 104) | Central Alabama (n = 127) | Worcester (n = 68) | all sites (n = 354) |
| **family-related** | | | | | |
| qualify for free lunch at school | 63% | 76% | 89% | 55% | 75% |
| "latchkey"–no adult home after school* | 40% | 24% | 20% | 18% | 27% |
| sibling dropped out of school** | 31% | 17% | 14% | 21% | 19% |
| adult at home "drinks a lot" | 11% | 8% | 9% | 3% | 8% |
| adult at home "takes a lot of drugs" | 11% | 12% | 6% | 5% | 8% |
| **neighborhood** | | | | | |
| have seen someone sell drugs near home | 4% | 31% | 28% | 20% | 24% |
| **participant risky behavior** | | | | | |
| skipped school, Spring 1988 | 4% | 8% | 3% | 13% | 6% |
| stole something, Spring 1988 | 0% | 4% | 0% | 4% | 2% |
| sexually active, Summer 1988 | 2% | 6% | 11% | 2% | 7% |
| **participant substance use** | | | | | |
| ever smoked cigarettes | 37% | 12% | 15% | 22% | 18% |
| ever drank alcohol | 46% | 27% | 30% | 28% | 31% |
| ever used other drugs | 17% | 16% | 16% | 12% | 15% |

*Percentage based on girls ages 11 and 12 only.
**Percentage based on girls with older siblings only.
Source: preprogram questionnaires; Smith & Kennedy (1991), Table 3

beginning–or continuing–substance use. On the preprogram questionnaire, one-third of participants (34%) reported previous use of one or more types of substances. More than half (52%) of all older participants (ages 13-15) reported substance use during the 10 weeks between completion of the preprogram and first postprogram questionnaires; by the third postprogram questionnaire more than three-fourths (78%) of older participants had reported substance use. For the younger participants, the percentage reporting at least one incident of substance use during the study period more than doubled, from 29 percent by the first postprogram questionnaire to 64 percent by the third postprogram questionnaire.

Friendly PEERsuasion appeared most effective in delaying initial or repeat substance use among the younger participants (Table 3). On the first postprogram questionnaire, when the treatment group had completed PEERsuader training, 22 percent of the younger girls in the treatment group versus 34 percent of the younger girls in the comparison group reported substance use since completing the preprogram questionnaire. Cumulated data for these participants from the first and the second postprogram questionnaires showed *no* increase in substance use among the treatment group (still 22%), while among the comparison group the cumulative percentage who reported using substances since the preprogram questionnaire increased to 40 percent ($p < .10$). Among the older participants, cumulative rates of reported substance use were virtually identical

TABLE 3. Cumulative Self-Reported Use of Any Harmful Substances Among Treatment Group (Fall 1988 Participants) and Comparison Group (Spring 1989 Delayed Entry Participants) Reported on First, Second or Third Postprogram Questionnaire, Stratified by Age, Friendly PEERsuasion, Birmingham, Alabama Site

| treatment group and age group | postprogram questionnaire | | |
|---|---|---|---|
| | 1 November 1988 | 2 February 1989 | 3 May 1989 |
| **younger (ages 11-12; n = 58)** | | | |
| treatment group (n = 23) | 22% | 22% | 52% |
| comparison group (n = 35) | 34% | 40%[a] | 71%[b] |
| **older (ages 13-15; n = 60)** | | | |
| treatment group (n = 24) | 54% | 54% | 79% |
| comparison group (n = 36) | 50% | 53% | 78% |
| **combined (ages 11-15; n = 118)** | | | |
| treatment group (n = 47) | 38% | 38% | 66% |
| comparison group (n = 71) | 42% | 46% | 75% |

[a]$p < .10$ ($r = .19$)
[b]$p < .10$ ($r = .20$)
Source: Chaiken et al. (1990), Tables H-1, H-2

for the treatment and comparison groups at the first and second postprogram questionnaires.

The younger girls in the treatment group remained significantly less likely than their peers in the comparison group to use substances even after both groups had participated in Friendly PEERsuasion (Table 3). Cumulating responses from all three postprogram questionnaires, 51 percent of younger girls in the treatment group but 71 percent of younger girls in the comparison group reported having used substances at least once during the study period ($p < .10$). This finding provides further evidence that the program was most effective for the youngest participants. As at earlier stages in the program, the rate of reported substance use by older girls in the treatment and comparison groups was virtually identical.

Younger girls participating in Friendly PEERsuasion were particularly likely to report leaving situations in which friends were using harmful substances (Table 4). After completing PEERsuader training, only 4 percent of the younger girls in the treatment group versus 14 percent of their peers in the comparison group reported staying in situations where peers were smoking, drinking or using other drugs. Eight weeks later, when the treatment group had completed teaching PEERsuade-Me's, still only 4 percent of this fall entry group versus 23 percent of the spring delayed-entry group reported staying while friends used drugs. By the end of the study period, when both groups had completed their participation in Friendly PEERsuasion, younger girls in the treatment group were still less likely than their peers in the treatment group to stay in a situation where peers were using substances. However, the gap between the likelihood for these two groups narrowed considerably, suggesting that given the chance to participate many of the later participants also "got the message." Once again, findings for older girls who participated in the program were similar for treatment and comparison groups.

Based on these findings Chaiken, Maltz and Smith recommended focusing programmatic efforts on preteen girls considered at very high risk for substance use. Replication and evaluation of Friendly PEERsuasion offered to additional girls from a variety of racial and ethnic backgrounds and living in risky circumstances would help to show if program impact could be duplicated or enhanced by other Girls Incorporated affiliates. They also suggested developing program components to continue the involvement of trained PEERsuaders as peer leaders in their communities, reasoning that girls who use the knowledge and teaching and leadership skills acquired through participation in Friendly PEERsuasion on an ongoing basis will be more likely to avoid future substance use and association

TABLE 4. Cumulative Self-Reported Failure to Leave a Situation in Which Peers Were Using Harmful Substances Among Treatment Group (Fall 1988 Participants) and Comparison Group (Spring 1989 Delayed Entry Participants) Reported on First, Second or Third Postprogram Questionnaire, Stratified by Age, Friendly PEERsuasion, Birmingham, Alabama Site

|  | postprogram questionnaire | | |
| --- | --- | --- | --- |
| **treatment group and age group** | **1** November 1988 | **2** February 1989 | **3** May 1989 |
| **younger (ages 11-12; n = 58)** | | | |
| treatment group (n = 23) | 4% | 4% | 17% |
| comparison group (n = 35) | 14% | 23%[a] | 29% |
| **older (ages 13-15; n = 60)** | | | |
| treatment group (n = 24) | 29% | 29% | 50% |
| comparison group (n = 36) | 31% | 33% | 44% |
| **combined (ages 11-15; n = 118)** | | | |
| treatment group (n = 47) | 17% | 17% | 34% |
| comparison group (n = 71) | 23% | 28%[b] | 36% |

[a]$p < .10$ ($r = .25$)
[b]$p < .05$ ($r = .13$)
Source: Chaiken et al. (1990), Tables H-1, H-2

with substance-using peers themselves while continuing to help younger children acquire the knowledge, skills and attitudes to do the same.

## EVALUATION PLAN–FOUR SITES
### (Smith & Kennedy, 1991)

Abt Associates evaluators Christine Smith and Stephen D. Kennedy, Ph.D. combined data from all four demonstration sites in their evaluation of the Friendly PEERsuasion program. This provided a beginning sample of 152 girls assigned to the treatment group and 202 to the comparison group. Attrition was 18 percent for the first postprogram survey and higher yet for the following two surveys. Based on the information provided in the preprogram survey, Smith and Kennedy found no evidence of differential attrition between the fall and spring groups. For both groups, they found some evidence of association between attrition and each of two background factors: seeing someone selling drugs near the respondent's home and past cigarette smoking.

*Program recruitment.* The Pinellas, Rapid City and Worcester affiliates recruited girls in grades 6 through 8 among their memberships and at local schools. Girls who completed the preprogram questionnaire were randomly assigned to fall and spring (delayed entry) groups. Participants included a geographically, racially and ethnically diverse group of girls (Table 1). These girls were considered to be at high risk of early substance abuse, although particular risk factors varied considerably by site (Table 2).

*Program implementation.* The three additional affiliates all offered Friendly PEERsuasion after school hours. In Worcester and Rapid City Friendly PEERsuasion was offered at the schools participants attended; the Pinellas program was offered at Girls Incorporated centers. As a result attendance was lower and attrition was higher than in Birmingham. Many participants attended all 14 training sessions, but the average number of sessions attended was 9. PEERsuaders in the three additional sites reported liking and learning from about 90 percent of the activities. They were rated by their leaders as reasonably enthusiastic, averaging 7 to 8 on the scale of 0 to 10 (Girls Incorporated, 1991).

*Evaluation design.* Delivering the program under more challenging circumstances than did Girls Incorporated of Central Alabama, the three additional sites had more difficulty in adhering strictly to the evaluation design. A few girls at these sites participated in program sessions in both fall and spring. Further, some girls who completed the preprogram questionnaire, especially girls assigned to the spring comparison group, never attended a program session (Girls Incorporated, 1991). Overall, the early stage of program implementation and the variations from the evaluation design mean that the results of the combined evaluation (Smith & Kennedy, 1991) should be taken as suggestive only.

Despite the random assignment of participants to fall and spring groups, Smith and Kennedy found some differences by group in behaviors and attitudes at the preprogram survey. Also, the proportion of girls assigned to each group varied somewhat by site. Therefore, Smith and Kennedy (1991, p. 14) developed a logistic formulation including dummy variables for site, age (11-12 or 13-15 at the preprogram questionnaire), behavior reported on the preprogram questionnaire and fall or spring participation to estimate the difference in rates of substance use and failure to leave situations where peers were using substances if the comparison group had participated in PEERsuader training and teaching at the same time the treatment group did.

*Findings.* The results of the four-site evaluation suggest that participation in Friendly PEERsuasion helps girls to achieve, at least on a short-term basis, the desirable outcomes of avoiding substance use and leaving situations in which substances are being used, particularly where the substance being used is alcohol. Participation in Friendly PEERsuasion reduced both the onset of drinking among participants who reported never having drunk alcohol and the incidence of drinking among those who reported having done so on the preprogram questionnaire. The estimated effect of the program if both groups had participated in the program during Fall 1988 would be to halve the incidence of drinking, from the actual rate of over 10 percent to under 5 percent. Moreover, the effectiveness of participation in Friendly PEERsuasion on delaying alcohol use persisted over the study period. Among participants who reported never having drunk alcohol at the preprogram questionnaire, 22 percent of the treatment group versus 36 percent of the comparison group reported first use of alcohol on a postprogram questionnaire.

Fall participants were more likely to leave situations where peers were drinking alcohol than were spring participants. On the third postprogram questionnaire 18 percent of the comparison group reported staying in situations where people were drinking alcohol. Had the comparison group participated in the fall with the treatment group, it was estimated that this number would have been halved, to less than 8 percent. Further, after completing PEERsuader training a lower percentage of fall participants reported favorable attitudes toward drinking alcohol than did their peers who had not yet begun PEERsuader training.

Finally there was again some evidence that participation was more effective for younger participants. Younger girls who participated earlier were less likely to begin using harmful substances during the study period and also less likely to keep up associations with substance-using peers; older girls reported similar behaviors regardless of earlier or later participation.

## *DISCUSSION*

By delaying first or repeat substance use, Friendly PEERsuasion supports the longer-term goal of minimizing use of "gateway drugs" and reducing the likelihood that participants progress to increasingly risky behaviors (cf. Dryfoos, 1990; CASA, 1996; Wallack & Corbett, 1990). Similarly, while Friendly PEERsuasion was designed to change the behavior of PEERsuaders, the prevalence of substance use among very young children confirms the importance of providing a head start on substance abuse prevention to PEERsuade-Me's.

Some of the success of Friendly PEERsuasion seems attributable to the focus on leadership development, providing a sense of power and control over one's circumstances. Friendly PEERsuasion also demonstrates the efficacy of the life skills approach, with its emphasis on training in decisionmaking, assertiveness, refusal and communication skills when taught and practiced in context (cf. Ellickson & Bell, 1990, Howard & McCabe, 1990).

The evaluations of Friendly PEERsuasion parallel those of other substance abuse prevention programs in finding that continuing reinforcement is necessary to help young people counter the many sources, personal and societal, of expectations and enticements to use drugs (cf. Gerbner, 1990; CASA, 1996). Opportunities for PEERsuaders to continue to use what they have learned to benefit themselves and others are a high priority.

On the whole, the evaluations of Friendly PEERsuasion confirmed that the program takes the right approach to helping young women avoid substance use. Continuing research supports our goals of helping girls acquire the skills, attitudes and confidence to be leaders and teachers, to think critically about the blandishments of friends or media to use substances, to manage stress in healthy ways, to steer friendships towards positive activities and to leave situations where substances are being used. Still, much research leading to better prevention and intervention strategies remains to be done. We need to learn more about the substances young people use depending on their gender, race, class, community, disability and neighborhood; the connections between experimenting with substances, using substances, abusing substances, being addicted to substances and recovering from addiction or reducing use, and the connections between substance use and other risky behaviors; and the roles of advertising, popular culture and adult role models as they influence early adolescents' attitudes and behavior related to substance use.

Friendly PEERsuasion curriculum materials (Girls Clubs of America [Girls Incorporated], 1989a, 1989b) and training were made available to all Girls Incorporated affiliates in 1990. It has rapidly become one of the most widely implemented national Girls Incorporated programs, offered by approximately half of all affiliates each year. In 1996 affiliates reported serving over 6,000 PEERsuaders and over 15,000 PEERsuade-Me's. The promise of Friendly PEERsuasion is that something can work to help young women counter the media messages and role models promoting substance use and abuse by making and keeping commitments to avoid harmful substances and the peers who use them.

## REFERENCES

Bodinger-de Uriarte, C. & Austin, G. (1991). *Substance abuse among adolescent females* (Prevention Research Update No. 9). Portland, OR: Northwest Regional Educational Laboratory.

Brunswick, A.F. & Messeri, P.A. (1984). Origins of cigarette smoking in academic achievement, stress and social expectations: Does gender make a difference? *Journal of Early Adolescence, 4,* 353-370.

Chaiken, M.R., Maltz, M.D., & Smith, C. (1990). *Evaluation of Girls Incorporated's Friendly PEERsuasion program: A push in the right direction.* Indianapolis: Girls Incorporated.

Dryfoos, J. (1990). *Adolescents at risk: Prevalence and prevention.* New York: Oxford University Press.

Ellickson, P.L. & Bell, R.M. (1990). Drug prevention in junior high: A multi-site longitudinal test. *Science, 247,* 1299-1305.

Elliott, D., & Huizinga, D. (1984, April). *The relationship between delinquent behavior and ADM problems.* Paper presented at the ADAMHA/OJJDP State of the Art Research Conference on Juvenile Offenders with Serious Drug, Alcohol, and Mental Health Problems.

Gerbner, G. (1990). Stories that hurt: Tobacco, alcohol and other drugs in the mass media. In H. Resnik (Ed.), *Youth and drugs: Society's mixed messages* (pp. 53-127). OSAP Prevention Monograph–6 [DHHS Publication No. (ADM)90-1689]. Rockville, MD: U.S. Department of Health and Human Services, Public Health Service, Alcohol, Drug Abuse and Mental Health Administration, Office for Substance Abuse Prevention.

Gilligan, C. (1982). *In a different voice: Psychological theory and women's development.* Cambridge: Harvard University Press.

Girls Clubs of America [Girls Incorporated]. (1983). Health. In *GCA policy statements: April 1983.* New York: Author.

Girls Clubs of America [Girls Incorporated]. (1985). *Girl Power: Health Power. A health promotion program for preadolescent girls.* New York: Author.

Girls Clubs of America [Girls Incorporated]. (1988). *Facts and reflections on girls and substance use.* New York: Author.

Girls Clubs of America [Girls Incorporated]. (1989a). *Friendly PEERsuasion$^{SM}$: Curriculum guide.* New York: Author.

Girls Clubs of America [Girls Incorporated]. (1989b). *My Friendly PEERsuasion$^{SM}$ teaching kit.* New York: Author.

Girls Incorporated. (1991). *Evaluation of the Girls Incorporated Friendly PEERsuasion$^{SM}$ program: Monitoring program implementation in three field test sites, Fall 1988-Spring 1989.* Indianapolis: Author.

Girls Incorporated. (1996). *Prevention and parity: Girls in juvenile justice.* New York: Author.

Howard, M. & McCabe, J.B. (1990). Helping teenagers postpone sexual involvement. *Family Planning Perspectives, 22,* 21-26.

Jackson, B. (1982). *The ladykillers: Why smoking is a feminist issue.* New York: Continuum.

Johnston, L.D., O'Malley, P.M., & Bachman, J.G. (1986). Drug use among American high school students, college students, and other young adults: National trends through 1985 [DHHS Publication No. (ADM) 86-1450]. Rockville, MD: National Institute on Drug Abuse.

Johnston, L.D., O'Malley, P.M., & Bachman, J.G. (1995). *National survey results on drug use from the Monitoring the Future study, 1975-1994. Volume I: Secondary school students* [NIH Publication No. 95-4026]. Rockville, MD: National Institute on Drug Abuse.

Kandel, D., Simcha-Fagan, O., & Davies, M. (1985). Risk factors for delinquency and illicit drug use from adolescence to young adulthood. *Journal of Drug Issues, 16,* 67-90.

National Center on Addiction and Substance Abuse at Columbia University [CASA]. (1996). *Substance abuse and the American woman.* New York: Author.

Perry, C.L, & Murray, D.M. (1985). The prevention of adolescent drug use: Implications from etiological, developmental, behavioral and environmental models. *Journal of Primary Prevention, 6(1),* 31-52.

Rousso, H. (1986). Confronting the myth of asexuality: The Networking Project for Disabled Women and Girls. *SIECUS Report, 14(4),* 4-6.

Smith, C., & Kennedy, S.D. (1991). *Final impact evaluation of the Friendly PEERsuasion targeted substance abuse education program of Girls Incorporated: A report on four demonstration sites* (available from Girls Incorporated National Resource Center).

Tobler, N. (1986). Meta-analysis of 143 adolescent drug prevention programs: Quantitative outcome results of program participants compared to a control or comparison group. *Journal of Drug Issues, 16,* 537-67.

Wallack, L. & Corbett, K. (1990). Illicit drug, tobacco, and alcohol use among youth: Trends and promising approaches in prevention. In H. Resnik (Ed.), *Youth and drugs: Society's mixed messages* (pp. 5-29). OSAP Prevention Monograph–6 [DHHS Publication No. (ADM)90-1689]. Rockville, MD: U.S. Department of Health and Human Services.

# The Nee-kon Project:
# Designing and Implementing
# Prevention Strategies
# for Young Native American Children

Barbara Laquer, MEd

SUMMARY. Demonstration programs creatively and adaptively deal with environmental factors which place children at high risk for later development of substance abuse. This article focuses on an example of such a program, designed to build resiliency and protective factors within young at-risk Indian children in Oklahoma through helping them bond to supportive adults and to school. Preschool children enrolled at the Kickapoo Head Start Center were involved in school transition, school readiness, school attendance, and classroom-based prevention activities while attending the Head Start Center and after matriculation into local public schools. Additional early intervention was provided to children already experiencing school adjustment difficulties. Families and Head Start staff were involved in interventions designed to make home and school environments more supportive. The article identifies the problems

Barbara Laquer is Senior Program Development Specialist at the American Indian Institute, College of Continuing Education, University of Oklahoma.

Address correspondence to: Barbara Laquer, Senior Program Development Specialist, American Indian Institute, College of Continuing Education, University of Oklahoma, 555 Constitution Street, Suite 237, Norman, OK 73072-7820.

The contents of this article are the sole responsibility of the author and do not necessarily represent the official views of the funding agency.

[Haworth co-indexing entry note]: "The Nee-kon Project: Designing and Implementing Prevention Strategies for Young Native American Children." Laquer, Barbara. Co-published simultaneously in *Drugs & Society* (The Haworth Press, Inc.) Vol. 12, No. 1/2, 1998, pp. 23-37; and: *Substance Abuse Prevention in Multicultural Communities* (ed: Jeanette Valentine, Judith A. De Jong, and Nancy J. Kennedy) The Haworth Press, Inc., 1998, pp. 23-37. Single or multiple copies of this article are available for a fee from The Haworth Document Delivery Service [1-800-342-9678, 9:00 a.m. - 5:00 p.m. (EST). E-mail address: getinfo@haworth.com].

*23*

constituting risk factors, details the culturally appropriate solutions generated and challenges met in the course of implementation. *[Article copies available for a fee from The Haworth Document Delivery Service: 1-800-342-9678. E-mail address: getinfo@haworth.com]*

## INTRODUCTION

In 1990, the American Indian Institute (AII), a department within the College of Continuing Education at the University of Oklahoma, was funded by the Center for Substance Abuse Prevention (CSAP) to undertake a five-year demonstration focusing on children who attended the Kickapoo Head Start Center located near McLoud, Oklahoma. A pre-demonstration needs assessment indicated that these children were at very high risk for developing two problems, school failure and use of alcohol and other drugs, which have been shown by the literature (Hawkins et al., 1985) to be related. Already at this preschool stage, many children were demonstrating precursors of future school failure, such as acting out, moodiness and learning difficulties. Parental involvement was low; many of the Native American parents tended to be uninvolved in their children's formal education for such reasons as their not valuing schooling, lack of transportation and child care, shyness in groups, language barriers, perceptions that they did not have proper clothing to wear to school events and functions, and/or a preoccupation with the basic food, clothing and shelter survival needs of their families. According to Hawkins and Weiss (1985), the bonding of youth at an early age to school and to significant others would form a protective factor reducing substance abuse.

In developing its early intervention component, the Nee-kon Project borrowed very heavily from the Primary Mental Health Project (PMHP), a research-based initiative headquartered in Rochester, New York. PMHP was formed in response to problems arising as a result of under staffing of school mental health services. In such situations, relatively minor problems experienced by children in the early grades are often ignored, take up a disproportionate amount of teachers' time and often lead to later serious problems for the children (Cowen, 1978). PMHP focuses on the early detection and prevention of such school adjustment problems in over 125 school districts within the State of New York. Across the nation it is estimated that some 500 school districts now have interventions modeled after PMHP that serve thousands of children. In operation for some 37 years, PMHP aims at "reducing social, emotional and school adjustment problems and enhancing learning skills and other school-related competencies" (Primary Mental Health Project Inc., 1992).

This paper focuses on the context within which demonstration activities were carried out, major prevention strategies/activities that were developed to transform risk factors in this environment, and challenges that were faced during the implementation process.

## CONTEXT OF THE DEMONSTRATION

The Kickapoo Head Start Center (KHSC) is located north of the town of McLoud in a rural area about 30 miles east of Oklahoma City, and 45 miles from the American Indian Institute. Students who attended this preschool were drawn from a large catchment area of approximately 70 square transportation miles, covering portions of four central Oklahoma counties. This situation presented a challenge related to interacting with the various jurisdictions of available state and federal, and Indian and non-Indian, education, mental health, and social services agencies and organizations in the area.

Most of the 3- to 5-year-old Kickapoo Head Start Center students were Native American of varying degrees of Indian blood, representing such tribes as Kickapoo, Cherokee, Chickasaw, Choctaw, Creek, Seminole, Shawnee, Caddo, Otoe-Missouria, Kiowa, Navajo, Cheyenne-Arapaho, San Ildefonso and Cheyenne. Some of the Kickapoo children came to school speaking and understanding only their native language. Many of the children lived in single parent families or were being raised by a relative or foster parent. Many had a large number of older and/or younger siblings. The traditional Indian concept of the extended family was evidenced by grandparents, aunts, uncles and cousins being very involved in the lives of many of the children.

The children's families live scattered throughout this rural land area in housing units provided by the Absentee Shawnee Housing Authority, rental houses or mobile homes in small towns or houses located in very isolated areas reached only by unpaved roads. Economic conditions were rather bleak and the vast majority of target children's parents or guardians (hereafter referred to as parents) were economically disadvantaged; a number were on welfare and others were able to find and maintain only low-paying jobs because of limited formal education. Some parents were illiterate, some spoke limited English or only their native language and some did not own a telephone or a means of transportation. These families were very much preoccupied with making ends meet and addressing basic needs related to food, shelter and clothing. This situation was not unusual, for as Davis and McCaul (1990) have noted:

> Many educationally disadvantaged children and youth come from families who are struggling to survive–personally, socially and eco-

nomically. For many of them, their parents have had negative experiences related to their own school careers. Their formal school environment which they, based upon their own past experiences, *perceived* to be uncaring and/or ineffective.

## PROJECT IMPLEMENTATION

The name "Nee-kon," derived from the Kickapoo word for friend, was chosen for the project. A project office was established behind the Kickapoo Head Start Center, north of McLoud. In addition to the project director, the staff consisted of a community/parent specialist, an evaluation/early intervention specialist (who jointly managed the McLoud Office), three community development assistants (known as Special Friends), two external evaluators and an evaluation liaison. In addition to staff, consultants were used to provide staff and parent training, develop a culturally sensitive preschool-based prevention curriculum and train KHSC teachers how to most effectively use it, and provide cultural/interpretation services. Staff members engaged in direct services were Native Americans either from, or familiar with, the McLoud area and having backgrounds that enabled them to understand the families with whom they worked. The project staff received training from the state director of the Primary Intervention Program (PIP) of California, which was itself adapted from PMHP and introduced to that state in 1981.

A Nee-kon Project Advisory Committee was formed to provide opportunities for local people and agencies to have ongoing input into the demonstration's programmatic activities. On an ongoing basis, this committee reviewed the progress of the demonstration, shared ideas, made suggestions, and expressed their points of view. The 13 committee members included the KHSC director, head teacher and community representative; parents of target children; a public school teacher, Indian Education counselor and Indian Education tutor; a representative of the Absentee Shawnee Housing Authority, Indian Health Service Shawnee Clinic, and Oklahoma Department of Human Services; and the director of the American Indian Institute. In addition to their advisory function, this group helped to disseminate project information to their respective constituency groups.

## INTERVENTIONS

The set of interventions implemented was multifaceted. The Special Friends component focused on those KHSC children identified as being most in need of help, other interventions involved all of the preschoolers. A third set of interventions was designed to make changes in the home and school environments of the children.

## SPECIAL FRIENDS EARLY INTERVENTION FOR TARGETED CHILDREN

The Special Friends component was designed for children already having problems with school adjustment. This element was based on an adaptation of PMHP, the Primary Intervention Program (PIP) and modified with Native American content. PIP fosters healthy self-concepts and social skill development, identifies children's individual strengths and needs early and helps prevent the possible need for more extensive, specialized help in the future (Johnson, 1989).

Four to five weeks after the beginning of the school year, KHSC and public school teachers having target children in their classrooms were trained in the use of two standardized screening instruments developed and used by PMHP early intervention programs. Prescreening results determined which children would receive special early intervention services from the Nee-kon Project staff during that school year. The initial screening instrument used was the AML-Revised which includes items designed to identify general acting out behaviors, moodiness and learning problems. School adjustment difficulties were sometimes indicated in more than one of these areas. For children whose AML-R scores indicated a problem, teachers completed a second screening using PMHP's Teacher-Child Rating Scale (T-CRS). The T-CRS is more behavior-specific and its results were used by the Nee-kon Project staff in developing appropriate goals for each child. Comments provided by the child's parents/guardians and teachers were also considered during the goal-setting stage.

Each identified child was assigned a Nee-kon Project staff member who became the child's "Special Friend." The Nee-kon Project's Special Friends were Native American paraprofessionals who demonstrated personal maturity, had had relevant life experiences and were able to relate very well with target children and their families. Special Friends provided children with their undivided attention on a regular basis, in a setting where the children were free to select from and engage in a variety of activities. During their first few weeks together, efforts focused on building a bond between the child and his or her Special Friend. They met together in one of the specially designed Nee-kon Playrooms located in two buildings behind the Kickapoo Head Start Center. Each playroom was filled with child-sized furniture, books, games, manipulatives, an adult-sized rocking chair, tape recorder, feelings charts, etc.

After a child had been seen five or six times, the Special Friend did a prescreening on the child using the PMHP's Associate-Child Rating Scale (A-CRS). The child's remaining sessions were then structured to meet goals that were individually set for them such as decreasing aggressive behavior, increasing peer interaction, decreasing shy or withdrawn behavior, increasing their attention span, decreasing disruptive classroom behaviors and/or improving school work habits. Based on a child's particular needs, sessions were structured to build self-esteem within an atmosphere which encouraged the expression of feelings and ideas through conversation, creative play materials, books, and games.

Each child had two 30-minute sessions per week with their Special Friend during school hours. If circumstances dictated, some children worked on a daily basis with a Special Friend until a special problem or crisis was resolved. Following a schedule, Special Friends took children from their classrooms to specially equipped playrooms behind the KHSC. In most cases, sessions together were on a one-to-one basis; however, Special Friends also worked with some children in small groups to provide them with structured experiences emphasizing pro-social skills, group interaction and socialization. Because children were taken from their classroom for sessions, an activity was designed to address the predictable curiosity of children regarding where selected children went with their Special Friends. At the beginning of each school year, a puppet show was provided for KHSC children. Its purpose was to introduce all children to the playrooms where early intervention sessions would later be held. Small groups of students saw the puppet show provided in English and sometimes in Kickapoo by the Special Friends. The puppet show was followed by guided tours of the facilities and time was provided for the children to explore the playrooms. The sessions were seen as desirable; Special Friends were approached by children not selected for early intervention who begged to be allowed to go with them.

The Nee-kon Project began work with its target children while they were attending the Kickapoo Head Start Center (KHSC) and followed these students into elementary school. The elementary school students (grades K-2) were seen for one hour each week after school hours. They were picked up from school by the Nee-kon Project Special Friends, transported to the Nee-kon Project playrooms, and then taken home after their sessions. Those in need of increasing their social skills were usually seen by a Special Friend as part of a small group of two to four children. Both before and during the span of time when sessions were taking place, Special Friends maintained contact with children's parent(s) and teachers to collect additional information which could shed further light on the situations of the children. Sessions usually lasted for 15-25 weeks. After they had been completed, end-of-the-school-year post-screenings were done by the teachers and Special Friends using the AML-R, T-CRS and A-CRS instruments. The Nee-kon Project Special Friends also arranged field trips for the youngsters to which parents were invited. By the fourth year of the demonstration, participants included 60 students at KHSC and 70 former KHSC students who were in 37 different classes in seven participating elementary schools.

## SCHOOL READINESS/TRANSITION COMPONENT

During each school year cycle, the Nee-kon Project staff engaged in a variety of school readiness and school transition activities designed to help children set the stage for school success. In order to aid home-to-school transition, Special Friends rode the KHSC school vans for a week at the beginning of each school year to assist incoming three- and four-year-old children who were "leaving home" for the first time without a family member. After riding the school vans, the Nee-kon staff spent time in KHSC classrooms helping children become familiar with their new surroundings and assisting KHSC teachers, as needed, with students who needed some special attention. Special support and encouragement was also provided to parents feeling stress at having their 3- or 4-year-old child go off to school. Riding the school vans at the beginning of the school year served another purpose: that of helping the Nee-kon Project staff learn where all of the new children lived. Another beginning-of-the-school-year transition activity focused on providing assistance to children who were moving from half-day kindergarten to attending school on a full day basis.

School-to-school transition activities began late each spring. Children about to graduate from KHSC were taken on field trips to the local public schools they would be attending in the fall. It was left to the discretion of participating schools as to how they wished to accommodate this transition activity, and procedures tended to differ from school to school and from teacher to teacher. During the 1993-94 school year, for example, one school had some former KHSC students provide the incoming KHSC group with a tour of their school. As visiting children were observing one kindergarten classroom in action, they were invited to take part with the class in a fishing game that involved identifying colors. Teachers at another school preferred that the children come when classes were not in session so that they would have more time to meet the children, show them around and allow them time to look around and play in the kindergarten classrooms.

During the summers, several activities were held for recent graduates of KHSC about to enter kindergarten. A five-day "Nee-kon Project Let's Get Ready for School Summer Session" provided children with a review of school-related skills. During these sessions, Special Friends engaged the children in a series of interesting and fun activities designed to help them get ready to enter kindergarten. These activities focused on a review of colors, shapes, numbers and other things useful for them to know as they entered school. The children were given opportunities to practice listening skills, follow directions and apply other school-related social skills. They also took part in music, art and movement activities, and discussed feelings about going to school for the first time. Transportation, breakfast and lunch were provided.

Before school started in August, children about to enter kindergarten were invited to attend the "Nee-kon Salon." Accompanied by a parent, each participating child received a hair cut and/or got a permanent wave from a Native American hair stylist. As the beautician cut or permed a child's hair, she taught the accompanying parent skills related to fixing the child's hair themselves. A mock "beauty parlor" was set up at the KHSC, chairs were arranged for waiting (with magazines available to browse through), and the Nee-kon staff took advantage of the opportunity to give the children school-related pep talks. Parents were provided with suggestions about how they could help their children make a smooth transition into public school. In one case, this intervention had an unintended impact in developing a parent's career; encouraged by the hair stylist, one mother entered and graduated from a school of cosmetology.

For children entering kindergarten, Nee-kon Project staff members were present at their respective schools during the first days of school, providing smiles and friendly faces to greet them when they arrived. Based on Nee-kon Project staff reports and teacher comments, the vast majority of students were able to make smooth transitions with few problems. A number of the kindergarten teachers expressed their gratitude to Nee-kon staff members for their contribution in aiding this transition.

"Back to School Reunions" were held each year before the beginning of school for Nee-kon Project cohorts about to enter first, second, or third grade. Because, after leaving KHSC, these youngsters ended up in many classes and schools, these "reunions" provided a good opportunity for them to visit KHSC and get together with their former KHSC classmates.

Clothing budgets were limited for many of the families. At the annual Christmas party, the Nee-kon Project provided gifts of a T-shirt or sweatshirt imprinted with the Nee-kon Project logo to each student and KHSC staff member. Christmas shirts for children in the public schools were usually in their school colors, and were delivered to them at home. Area public schools often sponsored "School Spirit Days" when children were supposed to wear their school color. This Nee-kon initiative ensured that target children would have something appropriate to wear on such occasions. Staff also helped resolve problems which arose. For example, it was learned that one of the target children, beginning kindergarten, was being teased at school by some of his classmates because of his long hair. The child's Special Friend (a Native American man who wears his hair long) arranged to make cultural presentations at the boy's school for the Johnson O'Malley Indian Education Committee and for the morning and afternoon kindergarten classes. Designed to help adults and the child's kindergarten classmates understand aspects of Indian culture (including the significance of males wearing their hair long), his presentation also included having the little boy and his older cousin do some traditional Indian dancing. This intervention not only brought an end to the teasing but also helped the boy's classmates develop a greater appreciation for him and his culture.

Over time, ongoing observations at participating schools enabled the demonstration staff not only to establish good working relationships with teachers, parent volunteers, counselors, aides, principals and secretaries, but also to observe target children in their school surroundings. This provided important information that guided the planning of Nee-kon activities in ways that best blended with children's regular school activities.

## SCHOOL ATTENDANCE COMPONENT

Native American children in the area tended to have very poor school attendance. Therefore, the Nee-kon Project sponsored an ongoing School Attendance Awards Program for its "target" children and their families during each school year. This focused attention on the importance of children attending school every day and developed or reinforced awareness among parents that attending school regularly was necessary related to their children's success in school.

The Nee-kon Project scheduled school attendance awards events for KHSC children after each quarter of the school year, and four times each school year for KHSC graduates attending elementary school. A Nee-kon Project staff member regularly verified children's school attendance with designated representatives at KHSC and each of the participating public schools. Students earned awards from the Nee-kon Project based on their attendance records of perfect (no absences), very good (maximum of one unexcused absence or two excused absences), or good (maximum of two unexcused, one excused and two unexcused, or four excused). It was soon noted by school staff that attendance improved and parents began to call in to explain absences.

School attendance awards events were held at the Kickapoo Head Start

Center during the early evening hours. Flyers announcing upcoming events to families who qualified for awards were disseminated ahead of time, home visits were scheduled to let children and their parents know about the event, and "reminder" telephone calls were made on the days that events were held. Transportation was provided to families on request, and child care was made available on-site. Children and their parent(s) were called to the front of the room for the presentation of awards. Gifts were provided both to children with qualifying attendance records and to their parents. The awards for the children were usually educational in nature such as school supplies, back packs, books, coloring books/crayons, toys and games. Gifts for parents were usually practical items that could benefit the entire family, such as frames to hold multiple pictures, towels, kitchen supplies, fire alarm devices (one family credited their device to later saving their lives), fire extinguishers and alarm clocks. During the presentation of awards at a school attendance event, group photographs of the children and their parents or guardians were often taken. News articles and photographs were developed for the local newspaper.

After the presentation of awards, there were drawings for the evening's door prizes. Everyone who attended an event received door prize tickets for signing an attendance list. This procedure enabled the program to maintain very accurate records of participation at these events. Door prizes were sometimes donated by local merchants. At other times, the Nee-kon Project provided a food box if the event was held at the end of a month (containing, for example, flour, sugar, bread, cereal, peanut butter, canned tuna, milk, meat, vegetables and fruit), or a box of useful household supplies (e.g., detergent, cleaning supplies, paper towels, toilet paper, soap, toothpaste, toothbrushes, bleach, dish cloths), if the event occurred at the beginning of a month. Sometimes drawings were also held for children's door prizes. Following the door prize drawings, a light supper was served buffet style featuring a traditional Indian meal or snacks. Families and the Nee-kon Project staff then had some time to socialize. KHSC staff members were often in attendance at the Nee-kon Project's attendance awards and other functions, just as the Nee-kon Project staff supported parent committee meetings, softball games and other events sponsored by KHSC.

## HOME VISITS COMPONENT

The Nee-kon Project staff made many visits to the homes of target children to confer with their parents or guardians. The purposes of these home visits were many and varied: to become acquainted with the families, to discuss children's school attendance, to provide parents with updates on their child's early intervention activities, to inquire how their child was doing in school, to collect evaluation-related information, to garner parent permission for their children to take part in activities, to let them know or remind them about upcoming Nee-kon Project activities, or to assist during a time of family crisis. The Nee-kon Project staff discovered that a visit to their home made target children feel very important. Perhaps just as significantly, the Nee-kons came to realize that some of the children's parents seemed to appreciate having a "Special Friend" as much as their children did. When the Nee-kon staff found no one at home while attempting to make a home visit, they left behind a message written on a "NEE-KON NOTE," carrying the Nee-kon logo so that the parents would know that they had stopped by. Such communication was necessary as many families didn't have telephones and thus could not be notified in advance of visits.

Other parent activities included a yearly Nee-kon Project Open House which provided an opportunity for parents or guardians to learn more about the demonstration and tour the project office and Nee-kon Playrooms. Support was also given each year to the KHSC Christmas party and graduation.

Parenting training was provided. A child guidance/parenting specialist provided well-attended talks entitled "How to Handle Stress During the Christmas Holidays: Tips and Tricks for Parents," and "Parenting: Ways to Make It Fun and Simple." A small group of parents were also taken to Oklahoma City to attend a summer series of parenting workshops. Most parent training occurred on a one-to-one basis with parents, often in conjunction with home visits.

The Nee-kon Project sponsored an American Red Cross Baby-sitting Course for the older brothers and sisters of the demonstration's target children. This was arranged after the staff realized that parents of target children often left them and their younger siblings in the care of their older 9- to 17-year-old children. Some of the participants reported that receiving their certificate later helped them get baby-sitting jobs outside their family.

The Nee-kon Project staff had thousands of contacts with parents of target children (including home visits, office visits, written correspondence and telephone contacts). As a result, the demonstration staff came to know many of these families much better than their KHSC or public school teachers, who often turned to the Nee-kon staff for information. Upon occasion, Nee-kon staff became involved in mediating problems parents were having with courts and other agencies.

Each year for KHSC graduation, the Nee-kon Project staff helped with the food for the reception following the ceremony and also videotaped the proceedings. Multiple copies of these videotapes were made and a copy was given to the family of each "graduating" child. The Nee-kon Project staff was supportive of the KHSC parent committees who planned and implemented this event and the annual Christmas party, attending fundraising functions and providing food and technical assistance.

## SCHOOL-BASED PREVENTION COMPONENT

In an effort to institutionalize the use of a preschool prevention curriculum within the Kickapoo Head Start Center, available curricula were reviewed, including those specifically designed for Native American children. It was determined by the Nee-kon Project staff and KHSC teachers that none met the most pressing needs of KHSC children. After the Nee-kon Project and KHSC staffs determined some of the desired content, *NEE-KON TIME: Prevention Activities for Preschoolers* was developed by consultant Sandra Gjelde for the American Indian Institute. It addresses prevention- and mental health-related developmental issues, focuses on how children feel about themselves and seeks to help them adjust and bond successfully to school.

In August 1992, a draft version of *NEE-KON TIME* was printed, and lessons/activities were subsequently piloted by KHSC teachers in their classrooms. At the end of the fourth year of the demonstration, the curriculum was edited and slightly expanded, based on input from the piloting teachers. The final version of what came to be called *NEE-KON'-NAH TIME* consists of 62 lessons/activities for large and small groups of children under the following headings: The Child and Family, Native American Culture, Recognizing Feelings, Receiving Positive Feedback, Self Help Skills, and Communication and Friendship Making Skills. Also provided is an introduction describing how materials blend with and address mandated components of the Head Start curriculum, a bibliography of children's books recommended for use with selected *NEE-KON'-NAH TIME* lessons and activities, and lists of supplies or resources needed to implement activities. A section entitled "Private Nee-kon'-nah Time" provides teachers with resource information in identifying and seeking assistance for children who are struggling to cope with matters such as: parental divorce, having a stepparent, death of a family member, foster family and/or adoption issues, living with grandparents and other guardians, and incarceration of a family member.

During the process of developing, piloting and refining *NEE-KON'-NAH TIME* materials, the developer provided inservice training for the KHSC staff in effectively implementing these lessons and activities in their classrooms. Most of the teachers had limited educational levels and little prior teaching experience. Like many other such programs, the Kickapoo Head Start Center was committed to providing a number of positions for the parents (most often mothers) of the children who attended school there. This built their self-confidence while providing them with the opportunity to learn work-related skills which could lead to other higher-paying positions. The best opportunity for the Nee-kon Project to assist teachers with their basic teaching and classroom management techniques was in conjunction with *NEE-KON'NAH TIME* inservice trainings which occurred twice each year.

The final version of *NEE-KON'-NAH TIME: Prevention Activities for Preschoolers* (1995) was completed and printed in time for use during the final Kickapoo Head Start Center school year of the CSAP demonstration. It has now been widely disseminated to American Indian and Alaska Native Head Start Centers for use across the country.

## CHALLENGES OF WORKING WITHIN THIS CONTEXT

The project staff had to be extremely flexible. Many parents had to operate on almost a day-to-day basis, and plans needed to take this into account. A number of the target families changed addresses frequently; tracking or locating them was aided by the staff's ongoing communication with parents through home visits and telephone contacts; an open door policy at the McLoud Office where parents were always welcome to stop by; and consistent, ongoing, personalized attention given to target children and their families. When cultural matters such as a funeral or adoption took place, other activities came to a halt within the most traditional segments of the Indian community. School cancellations during the winters due to snow or icy road conditions were a yearly reality, and extended school closings disrupted schedules of activities. All these elements made long-range planning difficult, and forced the staff to approach most activities with an implementation Plan A, Plan B and Plan C.

It was necessary to be aware of and sensitive to community conflicts, tribal politics, and long-standing feuds among local families. The staff committed themselves to adhering to strict standards of confidentiality, and tried to avoid becoming involved in gossip and nonproductive quarrels, disputes, and controversies. It required sensitivity, trustworthiness, persistence and demonstrated care for the target children and families in order for the local community to accept the demonstration staff, the "outsiders" from the University of Oklahoma.

By the end of the project, the program was working with 32 teachers in seven elementary schools as well as the KHSC. Changeover in staff and administration in these institutions necessitated ongoing work on relationships and familiarity with these educational institutions and the political, economic, and cultural contexts in which they operated. Changes in school populations and policies required modifications of the program. A written "working understanding" between the American Indian Institute and each of the participating schools was developed for each year of the demonstration. Signed by the school principals, American Indian Institute director, and project director, these documents detailed all demonstration-related activities and expectations involving the schools over the school year. This was found to be a very effective method of preventing potential misunderstandings and problems concerning what was to be done, who was responsible for doing what, and how activities were to be accomplished.

## CONCLUSIONS

The Nee-kon Project successfully implemented interventions which were needed by and benefited the target group of preschool children. Much was learned and reported to CSAP regarding the conditions that lead to the long-term survival of prevention programs in Indian/Native communities and the political, social, and other structural elements that support or hinder programs. The *NEE-KON'NAH TIME* curriculum developed by this program is being widely disseminated to Head Start Centers serving Native American children across the country.

It became clear to the staff over time, however, that while this effort successfully addressed school bonding, individual adjustment, and school environment elements, this effort was not comprehensive enough to make a major impact on the serious home environment problems that faced the target population. Over the course of the demonstration the mother of one "target" child committed suicide, the father of another child was beaten to death (inhalant abuse-related) and yet another father stabbed a relative to death (alcohol-related) and was incarcerated. Approximately 50% of the target children were children of substance abusers, about 20% were victims of abuse or neglect and some 20% had experienced domestic violence. These events underscore family risk factors and community risk factors that might have been more specifically addressed as part of a more comprehensive approach to prevention. This program was made possible by outside funding, and bringing in "outsiders" to the community, with the expertise to provide local people with support to carry out the intervention. As this funding terminates, so too will activities that took place under its auspices. This is probably the most unfortunate and all too likely outcome for prevention activities that can not be sustained by a broader community initiative.

# REFERENCES

Cowen, E. L. (1978). The primary mental health project: A prevention program. *Impact, 14,* 4-10.

Hawkins, J. D., Lishner, D. M., Catalano, R. F. Jr., and Howard, M. O. (1985). Childhood predictors of adolescent substance abuse: toward an empirically grounded theory, *Journal of Children in Contemporary Society, 18*(1/2), 11-48.

Hawkins, J. D. & Weiss, J. (1985). The social development model: an integrated approach to delinquency prevention. *Journal of Primary Prevention, 6*(2), 73-97.

Johnson, D. B. (1989). *A community in retrospect* (Annual Report of the Primary Intervention Program 1988-1989). Sacramento: California Department of Mental Health.

Nee-kon'-nah Time: Prevention activities for preschoolers (1995). Norman, Oklahoma: American Indian Institute.

Primary Mental Health Project Inc. (1992). *Annual report for the fiscal year ended June 30, 1992.* Rochester, NY.

# Evolution of a Substance Abuse Prevention Program with Inner City African-American Families

Georgia B. Aktan, PhD

SUMMARY. Substance abuse prevention programs successfully implemented and shown to be effective through rigorous evaluation must be able to respond to participant needs and changing environments in order to sustain themselves. The Safe Haven Program for the Prevention of Substance Abuse, a family skills training program for African-American families, is presented as an example of a substance abuse prevention program which evolved over time while the goals of the program remained stable. The author presents the program in a series of evolutionary stages: Program Implementation;

Georgia B. Aktan is Principal Investigator of the Safe Haven Program, City of Detroit Department of Health, Bureau of Substance Abuse; and Research Coordinator for the Needs Assessment Studies, Michigan Department of Community Health, Center for Substance Abuse Services.

Address correspondence to: Georgia B. Aktan, PhD, Research Coordinator, Needs Assessment Studies, MDCH/CSAS, 3423 ML King Jr. Boulevard, P.O. Box 30195, Lansing, MI 48909.

The Safe Haven Program for the Prevention of Substance Abuse was funded by grant No. H86 SP01793 from the U.S. Government, Center for Substance Abuse Prevention, Substance Abuse Mental Health Services Administration. The program was implemented by the city of Detroit Department of Health, Bureau of Substance Abuse, Detroit, MI 48202. The opinions stated here are those of the author and do not necessarily reflect the views of the U.S. Government, Center for Substance Abuse Prevention, or the City of Detroit Department of Health.

[Haworth co-indexing entry note]: "Evolution of a Substance Abuse Prevention Program with Inner City African-American Families." Aktan, Georgia B. Co-published simultaneously in *Drugs & Society* (The Haworth Press, Inc.) Vol. 12, No. 1/2, 1998, pp. 39-52; and: *Substance Abuse Prevention in Multicultural Communities* (ed: Jeanette Valentine, Judith A. De Jong, and Nancy J. Kennedy) The Haworth Press, Inc., 1998, pp. 39-52. Single or multiple copies of this article are available for a fee from The Haworth Document Delivery Service [1-800-342-9678, 9:00 a.m. - 5:00 p.m. (EST). E-mail address: getinfo@haworth.com].

Process/Outcome Evaluation; Environmental Impacts; Cultural Specificity Evaluation; Cross-site Evaluation; and Future Development. The author emphasizes the need to respond to participant needs and changing environments to enhance sustainability and calls for flexible evaluation components to accommodate the dynamic nature of substance abuse prevention programs. *[Article copies available for a fee from The Haworth Document Delivery Service: 1-800-342-9678. E-mail address: getinfo@haworth.com]*

## INTRODUCTION

Oetting and Beauvais (1991) note that implementation, effectiveness and sustantation are three processes relevant to the success of substance abuse prevention programs. While successful implementation is a necessary but not sufficient condition for effectiveness and sustantation, successful implementation and demonstrated effectiveness are necessary but not sufficient conditions for program sustantation. Participant needs and changing environments can challenge a program's long term viability. Substance abuse prevention programs must be able to respond to these challenges in order to sustain themselves. The Safe Haven Program for the Prevention of Substance Abuse, a family skills training program for African-American families in Detroit, Michigan, is an example of a program which changed over a five year period in response to various environmental impacts while the goals of the program remained unchanged. The purpose of this paper is to describe the progression of the Safe Haven Program over time and the responses to various environmental impacts which enhanced sustainability. The progression is presented as a series of evolutionary stages from implementation to dissemination.

## BACKGROUND INFORMATION

### Program Description

The Safe Haven Program (Aktan et al., 1994) is a substance abuse prevention program for African-American families in the city of Detroit. The goal of the program is to reduce the risk factors and increase protective factors for substance abuse in families where a parent is a known substance abuser. The youth targeted by the program are the six to twelve year old children of parents who have been admitted for substance abuse treatment services.

The Safe Haven Program is a modification for inner city African-American substance-abusing families of the 14-session Strengthening Families Program (Kumpfer et al., 1989) developed for children of substance abusers (DeMarsh and Kumpfer, 1986). The program is composed of 12 weekly structured sessions designed to improve outcomes in 10 areas: parent's parenting efficacy; parent's bonding with the child; child's positive behavior; child's school performance; child's school bonding and associations with positive peers; family cohesion; positive family communication; family expressiveness and organization. Approximately 96 families per year have been served over a five year period resulting in a total of nearly 500 families served.

The program curriculum, which includes parent, child and family components, is carried out by trainers using the program manuals and video. The Safe Haven Program is comprised of three self-contained classes conducted simultaneously to have maximum impact on the risk and protective factors. These three courses are parent training, children's skill training and family skills training.

The parent training program is based on a model by which parents are taught more appropriate methods to cope with their children's problem behaviors and to increase the number of positive interactions between themselves and their children. The parents learn to target problem behaviors, ignore inappropriate behaviors, and reward and increase appropriate behaviors in their children. A training manual and a parent's handbook containing group exercises and homework forms for each of the twelve weeks are utilized. The manuals contain sections on communication, developmental age/stage appropriate behaviors and drug education.

The children's skills training is designed to teach a variety of prosocial skills such as coping with loneliness, making choices and living with the consequences, controlling anger, recognizing feelings and coping with peer pressure. There is also an alcohol and drug education section. A handbook containing these lessons for the twelve weeks is utilized, designed for the six to twelve year old audience.

The family skills training involves both the parents and the children as a family unit. The parent is taught to track and understand the child's emotions and behaviors. The "child's game" is intended to help the parent to develop empathy and enjoy their children in a non-punitive environment where the children are encouraged to express their feelings. Trainers model the positive behaviors; parents imitate the behavior with the child. The trainer is always present to provide immediate reinforcement and cuing of the appropriate behaviors. The parents learn to apply appropriate limit-setters and to reward good behaviors.

The primary significance of the Safe Haven Program is that it takes a family skills training program which has been reported to reduce risk factors and actual use in children of substance abusers (Harrison, 1994) and modifies it for use with an African-American urban population. A detailed description of the Safe Haven Program, including the target population, participant recruitment, program setting and program content is reported by Aktan (1995).

## EVOLUTIONARY STAGES

The six evolutionary stages of the program which will be presented in this article are: Program Implementation, Process/Outcome Evaluation, Environmental Impacts, Cultural Specificity Evaluation, Cross-site Evaluation, and Future Development. Program implementation (stage one) is an overview of the Safe Haven implementation process including organizational structure, employee screening, training, and the participant qualification process which was completed during the first year of operation. In stage two, the initial process and outcome evaluation is described with the results of the evaluation presented. Stage three includes various environmental impacts which resulted in changes in both the curriculum and the evaluation. Stage four details the cultural specificity evaluation and the resultant modifications to the program. In stage five, participation of the Safe Haven Program in the Center for Substance Abuse Prevention (CSAP) cross-site evaluation is detailed with resultant modifications to the evaluation component. Finally, stage six presents the proposed dissemination of the program to the city of Detroit treatment system.

## STAGE ONE: PROGRAM IMPLEMENTATION

### Organizational Structure

The first step in the implementation of the Safe Haven Program was the establishment of an organizational structure comprised of institutional, managerial and technical levels. The institutional level is comprised of the position of principal investigator who interacts with the external environment and maintains the flow of information and resources to the program. The managerial level is comprised of the project director who coordinates and controls the work flow, makes decisions, and deals with problems which arise in the work setting. The technical level is comprised of the program trainers who, utilizing the program materials, carry out the program curriculum. Linkages are composed of authority and rules, such as defined in the Safe Haven Policy and Procedures Manual.

## Employee Screening

All potential employees were carefully screened to determine their expected level of job satisfaction, in addition to their professional qualifications for the position, with satisfaction intrinsic to the work the most powerful determinant. A professional consulting group specializing in the Detroit African-American family was engaged to assist in the interviewing process. Their unique contribution was in identifying individuals culturally-sensitive to the local urban African-American community, specifically of low socioeconomic status.

## Training

All individuals trained in the Safe Haven Program were trained in the Safe Haven philosophy and curriculum. Training was conducted over a three-day period and involved follow-up observations several months later. All individuals successfully completing the training were given professional development credit. In order to allow for participatory management wherever possible, all employees of the Safe Haven Program are requested to provide feedback on how the program can be improved, including how it can be made more meaningful to the targeted population.

## Participant Qualification Process

The participant qualification process was determined and is as follows: if the client in treatment has children within the age ranges suitable for the program (6-12 years) and living within the city of Detroit, the client's name is placed on a list of potential candidates for the Safe Haven Program. The potential client is interviewed by the liaison to the program who describes the program philosophy and structure. The liaison gathers additional information about the family and assesses the client's level of interest and potential commitment to complete the twelve week program. If the liaison indicates that the client is interested and potentially committed to the program, he/she is interviewed by the program director. The program director, with the client, contacts the primary care-giver and others involved with the day-to-day care of the children. In the final qualifications step, all family members must acknowledge the importance of regaining stability in their families and commit to participating in the full twelve week program. Following this acknowledgment, they are given a tentative date for the first session.

## STAGE TWO: PROCESS/OUTCOME EVALUATION

The first evaluation of the Safe Haven Program involved a process evaluation comprised of satisfaction and attendance records and an outcome evaluation comprised of pre- and posttest measurements on a standardized test battery of the parents and children in the program.

## Process Evaluation

The process evaluation forms, comprised of satisfaction and attendance records, were completed by the trainers after every session using a five point rating scale. Satisfaction ratings completed by the trainers included: an overall rating of the session content, completion of material, leader delivery, group enthusiasm, appropriateness of presentation, usefulness of homework, flow of presentations, usefulness of activities, usefulness of particular session and difficulty of session. The attendance records consisted of trainer ratings of the participants on the following group interaction variables: attendance, promptness, completion of homework, attention and participation, amount of disclosure and sharing, appropriateness of sharing, supportiveness of others, interest level, motivation level and competency in concept taught. The different dimensions were selected based on the hypothesis that active participation in the group process might affect outcomes.

## Outcome Evaluation

The outcome evaluation component of the Safe Haven Program used a non-equivalent comparison, repeated measures, quasi-experimental design which included pre- and posttest parent and child interviews. The outcome evaluation instruments consisted of a parent interview schedule and a child interview schedule. The parent interview was comprised of questions on the child's school behaviors, the child's characteristics, family and friends, parenting attitude, alcohol and drug use and depression. Items are drawn from the Moos Family Environment Scale (Moos, 1974) and the Achenbach and Edelbrock Child Behavior Checklist. The child's interview contained questions on social acceptance, school attitude, emotional behavior, alcohol and drug behavior and attitudes, family relations and responsibilities, problem behaviors, parental response to problem behaviors, problem solving, peer resistance and self-concept.

## STAGE THREE: ENVIRONMENTAL IMPACTS

The program was successfully implemented and effectiveness demonstrated through the first evaluation. However, challenges arose which necessitated changes to the curriculum and the outcome evaluation component and led to the creation of a referral procedure and a code of behavior.

## Curriculum

The Safe Haven Program as initially implemented was comprised of fourteen weekly sessions; however, the extensive outcome evaluation component required an additional two sessions to administer resulting in a sixteen week total program cycle. The duration of the implemented Safe Haven Program (sixteen weeks) did not coincide with the duration of the treatment period (twelve weeks) at the residential substance abuse treatment center where the substance-abusing parent was receiving treatment. This resulted in the substance-abusing parent completing treatment and leaving the residential center before completing the Safe Haven Program. Once the substance-abusing parent left the center, it was more difficult to locate and transport the client to the Safe Haven Program. As the discontinuity between the program cycle and the treatment cycle appeared to affect the retention rate, the program cycle had to be reduced to twelve weeks to coincide with the substance-abusing parent's treatment cycle. In addition, client interest and potential involvement in the Safe Haven Program at the treatment center was unprecedented. It became apparent very quickly that parents in substance abuse treatment could be engaged in a family activity for the potential benefit of their children. Rapidly, the waiting list for the program grew to anywhere between 25 and 50 families (the program was designed to serve 96 families per year) and was increasing as word spread in the treatment center that a new program existed to "help the kids." If the sixteen week cycle were shortened to twelve weeks, more families could be served and the waiting list brought under control.

Feedback from the families participating in the program also led to changes in the curriculum, not only in the length of the program but the sequence of the sessions. Feedback from Safe Haven staff indicated that the families participating in the program were frustrated with the first session as it was comprised solely of the pretest outcome measurement. The families wanted to begin the program curriculum at the first session rather than wait until the second session, the following week. The participants requested that, not only should the evaluation battery be reduced so that the program curriculum would begin at the first session, but that the session on alcohol and other drugs (then session #8) be moved to session #1. The families wanted to begin the program with the session on drugs and reported frustration at waiting for what they considered to be the most important session. This resulted in a change in the order of the sessions, not only to move session #8 to session #1, but also to combine some other sessions to reduce the overall number of weekly sessions to twelve.

## Outcome Evaluation

Challenges also occurred concerning the administration of the outcome battery, not solely the time constraints. The Safe Haven staff had to be extensively trained in administration of the parent and child interviews which used scarce resources. The interviews could not be self-administered as originally planned as the reading level of the Safe Haven Program participants was unexpectedly low; therefore, the staff were required to read the questions to the participants. Many questions were confusing to the participants and had to be reread. Rephrasing questions began to occur which could call into question the validity of the measurement. It was determined that shortening the battery to include only the Moos Family Environment Scale (Moos, 1974) and the Achenbock and Edelbrock Child Behavior Checklist would obtain reliable information sufficient to determine significant changes in the families and allow sufficient time to begin the program curriculum at the first session.

Once the curriculum was reduced to twelve weeks to coincide with the substance-abusing parent's treatment cycle, the sessions rearranged to move the session on alcohol and drugs to the first session, and the outcome battery reduced to accommodate the first session, the retention rate increased to approximately 80% and remained stable thereafter.

### Referral Procedure

The program, as originally designed, included transportation to and from the program sites and the provision of a hot meal at every session. It was believed that transportation and food would remove significant barriers to participation. It became clear very quickly, however, that the families participating in the program had many needs which resulted in unanticipated barriers to participation. This became obvious one bitterly cold winter night when the van driver arrived at the home of one family to transport them to the program site and the children did not have appropriate clothing to wear. In response, the staff obtained warm clothing for the children from a local agency. This led to staff involvement in the identification and referral of a host of problems for all the families, including financial and medical. To facilitate this process and make it as efficient as possible, a referral procedure was developed and a resource directory produced containing the names of agencies in the area. A psychologist was contracted on a limited basis to provide consultation to the Safe Haven Program wherever necessary, especially in cases of possible child abuse and neglect. A positive byproduct of the referral process was an increase in the amount of communication between and among the Safe Haven Program, the treatment center, and other agencies. The Safe Haven staff began to know and understand the unique circumstances of each of the participating families. This seemed to increase staff empathy for the families. The families, in turn, reported to the process evaluator that they felt the staff "cared about them."

Many of the families had children too young to participate in the program which is limited by the age appropriateness of the curriculum to children between the ages of six and twelve years. In order to enhance participation, maternal care representatives were added to the Safe Haven staff to care for the non-participating younger children on-site while the rest of the family was engaged in the program activities. The additional cost incurred for the maternal care representatives was offset by a reduction in the cost of the meals provided for the families. The meals, initially catered, were later prepared and delivered by a member of one of the participating congregations without charge.

### Code of Behavior

A major emphasis of the Safe Haven Program is in reuniting and strengthening the family unit. At times, parents of the children, who may have had limited contact prior to the program, responded inappropriately to the opportunity to be reunited with their families. Examples of this were when parents mistook the opportunity to engage romantically. On the opposite end of the continuum, heated arguments would erupt frequently about topics tangential to the session topic. Both kinds of occurrences, although rare, necessitated the development of a Safe Haven Program code of behavior which was strictly enforced by the Safe Haven staff. Training was developed by and for all staff to cope systematically and consistently with all behavior which threatened the safety of the group or to disrupt the group process. It is important to note that the van drivers were included in the training as they were required to remain on-site throughout the duration of every session should a participant require transportation home prior to the end of the session. "Time-outs" were sometimes called by the staff and a participant removed from the premises until the next session. This occurred very rarely and was only warranted when the participant arrived intoxicated or became combative with family or staff members. Generally, the staff, trained as substance abuse counselors as well as the Safe Haven Program, could maintain order and redirect the discussion to the topic at hand.

## STAGE FOUR: CULTURAL SPECIFICITY EVALUATION

It has been argued (Nobles, 1984; King, 1985) that service delivery to African-Americans is doomed to failure when it does not recognize or build on the cultural integrity of the African-American community. Therefore, a cultural specificity and sensitivity process evaluation was conducted. The cultural specificity evaluation was conducted by a consulting firm specializing in the local African-American family. The purpose of this evaluation was to determine client and staff response to the program curriculum and materials and to elicit recommendations from families currently participating, former participants and staff as to how the program could be made more meaningful to the local African-American population. The process evaluation was conducted on-site and included observations of the program sessions as well as interviews with families and staff. Family interviews were conducted with individual families in private. Staff was interviewed both individually and as a group. Staff also completed written responses to a fixed set of questions. All responses from both the families and staff were anonymous.

Based on observations of the group process, the evaluator indicated that the families seemed to have difficulty identifying with certain terminologies and concepts, such as differential attention wherein the child's negative behavior is ignored. The evaluator theorized that such concepts are not consistent with African-American parenting styles. The participants responded positively to references of current strengths of the families with cultural references such as survival, use of extended family including non-blood relations, and spirituality. At these times, the families were observed to communicate more and appeared more at ease. In the interviews, the families reported favorable comments such as "I can be a better parent if I know I am already doing something right" and "it's O.K. to talk about God."

Interviews with staff revealed that, although they believed the general program model was effective in meeting the needs of the families, it did not embody the characteristics of an Afrocentric approach. Staff reported that certain concepts seemed to be antithetical to the African-American historical/cultural frame of reference such as the non-use of corporal punishment. In addition, the video and art work did not reflect an African-American heritage. The staff believed that the video and art work was not specific to the participants.

Some of the recommendations of the evaluator were the following: all pictures/illustrations and other visual aids should be culturally-specific; corporal punishment should be discussed from a historical/cultural framework as a viable but not all-inclusive alternative; and the model's didactical approach of presentation should be modified to enhance the responsiveness of the African-American participants. Based on this evaluation, the Safe Haven principal investigator, project director and developer of the Strengthening Families Program implemented the following modifications: an all African-American video was produced with original scripts based on typical family life situations encountered by families of local substance abusers; all art work utilized in the program manuals was redrawn to reflect African-American heritage; and certain concepts and terminology used in the program were revised to be more in line with the African-American historical/cultural frame of reference. The modified manuals and new video became the basis of the Safe Haven Program curriculum (Aktan et al., 1994).

## STAGE FIVE: CROSS-SITE EVALUATION

The Safe Haven Program participated in two site visits in 1994: a Center for Substance Abuse Prevention (CSAP) site visit comprised of three days of observation and consultation by the CSAP Project Officer; and the CSAP cross-site evaluation comprised of ten days of observations and information-gathering by three CSAP consultants with expertise in evaluation. The three-day site visit was comprised of a standard format wherein observations were made by the Project Officer; records, reports and data examined; and recommendations given on methods to enhance the effectiveness of the program or to solve problems. In contrast, the purpose of the cross-site evaluation was to conduct an evaluation, not simply within a specific program, but *across* approximately sixty programs to determine significant effects which might not be detected with small samples. In order to group like program interventions, a domain matrix was developed which demonstrated that youth grow up within a number of environments which can be conceptualized as domains: family, school, peer group, community and the larger society. For the cross-site evaluation, programs were clustered into groups of programs focusing on common domains. The Safe Haven Program was evaluated as part of a group of programs focusing on the family unit.

Both of these site visits involved the participation of the principal investigator, project director, Safe Haven staff, current families participating in the program and former participating families. Observations were made of the program in process. Numerous families as well as individuals contributed feedback on the program, i.e., how the program had personally benefitted them as well as how the program could be improved.

Participants testified to a variety of positive changes in their lives which they attributed to participation in the Safe Haven Program. One significant improvement in the families was reported by former substance-abusing parents who indicated that they felt more in control of their lives, received more support from their families, and had taken steps to resume their education or to locate employment. In some cases, the parent indicated that their confidence was enhanced, not solely in parenting, but in a general sense, which propelled them to seek and find employment. Some non-substance-abusing parents indicated that this freed them to focus more on the needs of the children and themselves. The parents also reported that the children's school achievement improved in terms of higher grades on report cards. It became obvious that there were multiple domain impacts resonating through the families' systems which the evaluation component was not designed to measure.

A revision of the evaluation component will be developed in the future contingent upon the acquisition of resources to support this effort. The purpose of the revised evaluation would be to measure these "snowball" effects which appear to reverberate beyond the targeted child to other areas of the family system, including possible enhancement of treatment effectiveness in the substance-abusing parent. The revised evaluation would determine, in addition to changes in family environment and child behavior, possible effects related to participation in the program such as use/relapse and employment information from interviews and treatment records.

## STAGE SIX: FUTURE DEVELOPMENT

The program will continue to require further development, however, to successfully meet inevitable challenges. An example of a significant future challenge is in the development of the program for dissemination throughout the city of Detroit treatment system. Some of the challenges involved in dissemination can be identified, such as variability across treatment programs; large scale training requirements; limited resources for transportation and child care; quality control; and logistical constraints. Other challenges will undoubtedly occur as the needs of participants or the environment require it.

## CONCLUSION

The Safe Haven Program has demonstrated that it is possible to engage substance-abusing parents in relatively lengthy parenting and family programs and keep them involved until graduation. The results of the process evaluation, which included frequent observations of training, staff meetings, and the family groups by the program originator and trainer, demonstrated that the Safe Haven Program staff were successful in recruiting families, implementing the program and collecting data necessary for the evaluation component of the project. Trainer ratings on session fidelity checklists, suggested by project staff, were true to the intent of the program. Although participant involvement was rated for each session by the trainers, it was not found to predict outcomes.

As reported in Aktan et al. (1996), results of the outcome evaluation indicated that the program was effective in several areas. Among the parents, parenting efficacy increased while depression and drug use decreased. As rated by the parents, children's externalizing behavior, aggression, depression, hyperactivity, and school problems decreased. School bonding and time spent together in parent-child activities increased. As measured by the Family Environment Scale, family cohesion also increased.

Nonetheless, the six evolutionary stages of the Safe Haven Program presented here demonstrate challenges which can and do occur in substance abuse prevention programs beyond the well-documented issues of implementation and effectiveness. The Safe Haven Program was successfully implemented and shown to be effective; however, other challenges occurred during the life of the program which posed real threats to the program's viability. These challenges necessitated actions on the part of staff to sustain the program and, in numerous instances, resulted in a stronger program than would otherwise have been the case. Flexibility in the management of programs is necessary to meet these types of challenges and evaluation components must remain flexible as well to accommodate the ever present changeability of programs.

## REFERENCES

Aktan, G.B. (1995). Organizational frameworks of a substance use prevention program. Int. J. Addict. 30(2):185-201.

Aktan, G.B., Bridges, S.D. and Kumpfer, K.L. (1994). The Safe Haven Program: Strengthening African-American Families. Children's Training Manual. Detroit Department of Health, Bureau of Substance Abuse.

Aktan, G.B., Bridges, S.D. and Kumpfer, K.L. (1994). The Safe Haven Program: Strengthening African-American Families. Family Training Manual. Detroit Department of Health, Bureau of Substance Abuse.

Aktan, G.B., Bridges, S.D. and Kumpfer, K.L. (1994). The Safe Haven Program: Strengthening African-American Families. Parent Training Manual. Detroit Department of Health, Bureau of Substance Abuse.

Aktan, G.B., Kumpfer, K.L. and Turner, C.W. (1996). Effectiveness of a family skills training program for substance use prevention with inner city African-American families. Substance Use and Misuse, 31(2): 157-175.

DeMarsh, J.P. and Kumpfer, K.L. (1986). Family-oriented interventions for the prevention of chemical dependency in children and adolescents. In Ezekoye, S., Kumpfer, K., & Bukoski, W. (Eds.) Childhood and Chemical Abuse: Prevention and Intervention. New York: The Haworth Press, Inc.

Harrison, R.S. (1994). Final evaluation of the Utah Community Youth Activity Project. Submitted to the Utah State Division of Substance Abuse. Social Research Institute, Graduate School of Social Work, University of Utah, Salt Lake City, UT.

King, L.M. (1985). Behavioral indices of alcoholism in a black community: research findings. Paper presented at the NIAAA Conference on the Epidemiology of Alcohol Use and Abuse among U.S. Ethnic Minority Groups. NIH, Bethesda, Md.

Kumpfer, K.L., DeMarsh, J. and Child, W. (1989). The Strengthening Families Program: Children's Training Manual. Department of Health Education, University of Utah and Alta Institute.

Kumpfer, K.L., DeMarsh, J. and Child, W. (1989). The Strengthening Families Program: Family Training Manual. Department of Health Education, University of Utah and Alta Institute.

Kumpfer, K.L., DeMarsh, J. and Child, W. (1989). The Strengthening Families Program: Parent Training Manual. Department of Health Education, University of Utah and Alta Institute.

Moos, R.H. (1974). Family Environment Scale. Palo Alto, CA: Consulting Psychologists Press, Inc.

Nobles, W.W. (1984). Alienation, human transformation and adolescent drug use: Toward a reconceptualization of the problem. J Drug Issues 14(2): 243-252.

Oetting, E.R., and Beauvais, F. (1991). Critical incidents: Failure in prevention. Int. J. Addict. 26(7): 797-820.

# Alcohol and Drug Prevention Among American Indian Families: The Family Circles Program

Kit R. Van Stelle, MA
Glory A. Allen, AA
D. Paul Moberg, PhD

**SUMMARY.** The goal of the Family Circles Program was the prevention or reduction of alcohol and drug abuse among American Indian High Risk Youth on the Lac du Flambeau Indian Reservation through cultural enhancement of their family systems. The project was targeted toward families of high risk youth, ranging from four to eighteen years of age. A family systems approach was utilized involving the entire family, children, adolescents, parents, and grandparents. A culturally-oriented curriculum was developed which emphasized American Indian values, beliefs, and practices, relating them to contemporary life. Factors which positively impacted the implementation of the Family Circles Program included the development of interagency linkages, the retention of staff committed to the

---

Kit R. Van Stelle and D. Paul Moberg are affiliated with the University of Wisconsin Center for Health Policy and Program Evaluation. Glory A. Allen is affiliated with the Lac du Flambeau Band of Lake Superior Chippewa Indians.

This study was supported by the Center for Substance Abuse Prevention (Grant Number 1H86SP02403-01) to the Lac du Flambeau Band of Lake Superior Chippewa Indians.

The contents of this article are the sole responsibility of the authors and do not necessarily represent the official views of the funding agency.

[Haworth co-indexing entry note]: "Alcohol and Drug Prevention Among American Indian Families: The Family Circles Program." Van Stelle, Kit R., Glory A. Allen, and D. Paul Moberg. Co-published simultaneously in *Drugs & Society* (The Haworth Press, Inc.) Vol. 12, No. 1/2, 1998, pp. 53-60; and: *Substance Abuse Prevention in Multicultural Communities* (ed: Jeanette Valentine, Judith A. De Jong, and Nancy J. Kennedy) The Haworth Press, Inc., 1998, pp. 53-60. Single or multiple copies of this article are available for a fee from The Haworth Document Delivery Service [1-800-342-9678, 9:00 a.m. - 5:00 p.m. (EST). E-mail address: getinfo@haworth.com].

*53*

program philosophy, and the evolution of the project into a compre-hensive and holistic system of services for the entire community. *[Article copies available for a fee from The Haworth Document Delivery Service: 1-800-342-9678. E-mail address: getinfo@haworth.com]*

## INTRODUCTION

American Indian people have been exposed to years of acculturation that have resulted in a damaged cultural self-esteem and feelings of apathy and helplessness. The unhealthy ways in which Indian families interact is directly related to self-perceptions, values, and self-esteem. Changing these feelings and behaviors begins with changing a basic sense of self-awareness. Traditional American Indian culture offers healthy alternatives to unhealthy acculturated behaviors, ideals, and values. The lives of American Indian families can be enhanced by providing them with the opportu-nity to learn how to replace dysfunctional ways of interacting with the nurturing ways of their traditional culture. Changing the unhealthy behav-iors and self-concepts of American Indian families requires a holistic approach of nurturing the spiritual, emotional, physical, and intellectual selves. In spite of all the challenges Indian families have faced throughout history, there is still a strong family allegiance. This is a fundamental and enduring aspect of the American Indian family that can be built upon to foster and sustain healthy family lifestyles.

## DESCRIPTION OF PROJECT

The Family Circles Program sought to prevent or reduce alcohol and drug abuse among American Indian high risk youth on the Lac du Flam-beau Indian Reservation in Wisconsin through cultural enhancement of their family systems. A family systems approach was utilized involving the entire family: children, adolescents, parents, and grandparents. A com-prehensive, coordinated, culturally-oriented program and curriculum were developed which related traditional Ojibwe values, beliefs, and traditions to contemporary life. Ojibwe language instruction, individual family out-reach meetings, family cultural gatherings, support groups, and special family cultural celebrations were also a part of the project activities. The project approach was one of reinforcing and facilitating healthy family functioning through the constructive cultural teachings of traditional Ojibwe tribal values, beliefs, and practices which are inconsistent with alcohol and drug abuse.

### Parenting Education Class Component

The Family Circles Program developed three different curricula to guide the weekly program classes: a 24-week program for adults (which was also adapted for adolescents), a 24-week children's curriculum, and an Ojibwe language curriculum. All of these curricula were developed in consultation with elders from Lac du Flambeau as well as other Ojibwe communities. The adult and children's curricula include information on Ojibwe culture and history, Lac du Flambeau history, development of the four aspects of self (physical, intellectual, emotional, and spiritual), development of communication and parenting skills, information on alcohol and other drug (AOD) abuse, and the dynamics of dysfunctional families.

A weekend retreat was held for the families before the start of each annual 24-week program cycle to introduce them to the basic philosophy of the program and engage in family-oriented cultural activities. Participants gathered each week thereafter at the Family Circles office to attend the two-hour parenting and cultural education classes that revolved around the cultural curriculum. These weekly classes provided for grandparents, parents, and youth were facilitated by Family Circles staff each week for 24 weeks. A Cultural Celebration was held for all families who completed the 24-week program.

Family Circles provided curriculum classes to 133 American Indian families over the five-year period, consisting of 217 adults and 227 youth ages 4-17 years. Families who completed the Family Circles curriculum attended an average of 16 classes. Drop-outs attended an average of nine classes, with 77 percent attending 12 classes or less.

### Ojibwe Language Component

Family Circles Ojibwe Language Classes were provided to give participants a more formal and real sense of native and tribal identity, to empower them by providing the opportunity to achieve greater levels of self-expression, and to provide them with the skills to effectively communicate about their culture and teach it to future generations. The language curriculum developed by the program was used by instructors and program participants as part of the Family Circles classes. The weekly one-hour language classes provided for adults, adolescents, and children were taught by the Ojibwe Language Coordinator and other Family Circles staff for each of the 24 weeks.

The Ojibwe language component also included the Assistant Ojibwe Language Trainee Program which was designed to address the retention of the Ojibwe language for future generations. The trainees were young, highly motivated, and showed a propensity for speaking the Ojibwe language. Each trainee received 12 hours of language training per week for 48 weeks each year.

### Home Visit Component

Bi-weekly family outreach meetings were held in the home of each participating family. The Outreach Coordinator made a pre-arranged home visit with each family as a follow-up to the weekly group meetings. These family outreach meetings facilitated retention of the families in the project by helping to meet any immediate needs they might have had. The home visit provided each family with an opportunity to clarify and discuss the material presented in the groups and to receive assistance with completion of outside assignments. The Outreach Coordinator also made observations of the family and assisted in referrals to AODA treatment, aftercare, financial counseling, family therapy, and medical services such as hearing testing and dentistry.

### Support Group Component

The Support Group was offered immediately following the completion of the parenting classes to provide families with the opportunity to participate in sixteen weekly alcohol- and drug-free family-oriented cultural activities. Family Circles staff organized activities that provided families with the opportunity to discuss and elaborate on curriculum material from the class sessions, as well as address relevant issues brought up by group members. In addition, family-oriented cultural activities were offered such as sweat lodge, fry bread contest, summer feast, domestic abuse presentation, gathering wild rice, and making birch bark baskets.

### Elders Resource Council Component

Tribal elders from the community were recruited to provide cultural guidance for the program and the families involved by serving on the Elders Resource Council. Family Circles staff nurtured the elders, strengthening both their ability and desire to take on the role of traditional cultural teachers. The elders provided language instruction, provided program staff with guidance on curriculum content at weekly staff meetings, conducted traditional ceremonies, and contributed additional cultural material not contained in the curriculum.

### Project Newsletter Component

*Family Circles,* a 24-page newsletter, was developed and distributed each month during all five years of the project. Articles and news items related to information about healthy lifestyles and strengthening the physical, intellectual, emotional, and spiritual self. *Family Circles* included news of positive events in the community, historical information about Lac du Flambeau, highlighted community youth who were positive role models, and addressed prevention and recovery issues through articles on alcohol and drugs, domestic and sexual abuse, and other aspects of achieving a healthy lifestyle. The philosophy of the program and much of the information provided to program participants was made available to the community through the newsletter with the publication of excerpts from the Family Circles curriculum and exercises in Ojibwe language.

### *Anishinabe Sports Program Component*

The Anishinabe Sports Program associated with Family Circles is a non-profit project funded through Billy Mills Running Strong for American Indian Youth and the Christian Relief Fund. This component addressed the development of the physical and emotional aspects of the self. It promoted family-oriented physical fitness activities that were open to all community members. Competitive runs and skiing events provided community youth with the opportunity to participate in competitive events in their own community, as well as to attract people from surrounding communities to Lac du Flambeau. These runs enabled individuals from outside Lac du Flambeau to learn about the community and helped to foster positive relationships between Lac du Flambeau and area communities.

### *Other Project Services*

A wide variety of other AOD-free cultural activities were also sponsored by Family Circles on an ongoing basis. Project participants took part in weekly potluck feasts, dancing, singing, special traditional ceremonies, and story-telling. Sweat lodge ceremonies, traditional purification and meditation practices were also available for families each month. Family Circles also sponsored a New Year's Eve Sobriety pow-wow and a NiiJii Sobriety pow-wow each year. The project also conducted a series of Project and Curriculum workshops to disseminate information about Family Circles. The purpose of the workshops was to market the Family Circles curriculum and promote the program concept to other Wisconsin tribes. Project staff also conducted school presentations on cultural competence to area teachers each year in efforts to increase the cultural awareness of educators serving tribal youth.

Process data were used to address participant attrition, and modify and improve the program services provided. Family Circles staff responded to the problem of attrition in a variety of ways. First, adequate time was made available for recruitment of families that demonstrated the strength to effectively participate in and complete the program. Second, additional families were recruited for participation as an added safeguard against attrition. Program staff also responded by modifying the scheduling and structure of Family Circles classes to accommodate cultural/seasonal events such as spearfishing, seasonal employment, and pow-wows. Classes were not held when there was a death in the community so that families could show respect for elders by attending funerals. Finally, staff responded to participant requests by scheduling more joint class activities for parents and youth to participate in *together.* Ojibwe language instruction also evolved over the course of the project. At first, written materials were emphasized, but the emphasis later shifted to development of oral communication and speaking skills. With the adults and children participating in language instruction together, new activities (such as games) were developed. Based on participant feedback, the focus of the support group sessions was changed from one emphasizing review of the 24-week curriculum with group discussion to one stressing participation in family-oriented cultural activities. The home visit component was also modified to better meet participant need. It quickly became apparent that some families needed fewer visits while some needed more, so the level of home visits was tailored to the needs of each specific family. It also became clear that the project needed to be sensitive to how many other community programs were doing in-home visits, and to limit Family Circles home visits accordingly.

## CONCLUSION

The Family Circles Program had a positive impact on the Lac du Flambeau community, its families, and its individuals. The project received national recognition for the development of its curriculum, and expanded its program services to involve the entire community. Family Circles played a vital role in the revival of Ojibwe language and culture on the reservation by significantly increasing the cultural and native language knowledge of participants. It reinforced positive feelings about being Indian and the importance of traditional family support systems, providing the community with the opportunity to participate in family-oriented alcohol- and drug-free activities.

An element critical to the success of this project was the quality and commitment of the project staff. This highly motivated group of local professionals was deeply dedicated to serving community individuals of all ages. They viewed their efforts not simply as jobs, but as a way to improve the community in which they lived. They consistently practiced the traditional Ojibwe customs and served as role models, working toward community change through active involvement in committees, boards, etc. The lack of staff turnover also positively impacted the project. All of the project and evaluation staff involved at the start of the grant were still involved with the project when it ended. This consistency in staffing provided continuity in service provision and sent a message of stability to the community.

Interagency linkages were vital to successfully delivering services and achieving project goals. The support of the tribal organizational and governmental structure proved to be particularly important to implementation of the Family Circles Program. Establishing cooperative relationships with human service programs, health programs, schools, and tribal elders directly contributed to the success of the program. Tribal communities who seek to replicate Family Circles should build onto and coordinate with their own local programs.

The importance of developing a strong partnership between program and evaluation staff was also confirmed. The evolution of the evaluation of the Family Circles Program taught us that evaluations should incorporate an approach aimed at program improvement, staff ownership, and empowerment. American Indians have, historically, participated in research and evaluation endeavors in which they have provided information to outside evaluators and received very little benefit in return. We believe that a successful evaluation includes an effective *interactive* partnership among program staff, service providers, and evaluation staff. Projects of this type require an evaluator with both the expertise to provide the appropriate technical assistance and the cultural competence necessary to interact effectively with program staff. Although program staff were initially quite resistant to the idea of evaluating the program, the development of a trusting relationship with evaluators fostered an understanding of the benefits and uses of evaluation. Project and evaluation staff learned a great deal from each other, developing a partnership that both enhanced the implementation of the evaluation and allowed the evaluator to be part of the project team.

One of the most significant things demonstrated was the importance of retaining the flexibility to modify the program based on participant feedback. Evaluation data were used for program improvement in a variety of ways, and Family Circles was constantly modified to meet the changing needs of the participants. Program staff were extremely responsive to participant feedback regarding class scheduling, curriculum content, and presentation format. Many of these modifications involved changes in class schedules to aid in participant recruitment and retention, while others improved the quality of the programming by making it more family-oriented. As a result, the program continued to grow and evolve over the course of the project.

Efforts to replicate this or similar projects should incorporate a culturally appropriate concept of "family" into the design of both the program and the evaluation prior to implementation. The definition of "family" is a fluid and broadly inclusive concept for this population. The concept of family is not necessarily limited to blood relationships or shared living situations, but is more often expanded to include friends, elders, clan affiliations, and the tribal community as a whole. This enhanced notion of "family" resulted in a high level of movement of individuals between family units (a more circumscribed definition of family imposed by funders and evaluators). The project experienced difficulties in communicating the implications of this concept to funders, particularly with regard to the appropriate number of "families" to serve each year and the development of project goals and objectives.

Family Circles impacted the entire Lac du Flambeau community, not just those who participated in the classroom curriculum. The project grew to become a *community* program, coordinating with other tribal service providers and reaching out to touch tribal families in myriad ways. Family Circles networked with sober parents through tribal Alcoholics Anonymous groups, Head Start, and local schools to coordinate activities. The project expanded to operate the Anishinabe Sports run/walk and cross-country ski programs. The monthly project newsletter and posters in community gathering places provided cultural and language information to the community at large. Project staff conducted school presentations on cultural competence to area teachers each year, and offered feasts, ceremonies, pow-wows, and dances that were open to the entire community. Staff and project elders were extremely active and visible in the community outside of their work roles, serving on committees, performing traditional ceremonies, and providing cultural expertise. The joint impact of these numerous efforts was one of a ripple effect–with repercussions that spread both formally and informally from one community member to the next. Family Circles grew to receive recognition and acceptance exceeding our expectations, sowing the seeds of a community-wide revival of traditional Ojibwe culture.

# Impact of a Family and School Based Prevention Program on Protective Factors for High Risk Youth

Lynn McDonald, ACSW, PhD
Thomas V. Sayger, PhD

**SUMMARY.** The paper presents an overview of a multifamily based prevention program for at-risk youth, Family and Schools Together (FAST) and results of research conducted on program outcomes. Results are presented on three different phases of a research design, post, 6 month and 2 year follow ups. These data suggest that FAST is effective from pre- to post-participation in increasing both child functioning and family cohesion. The data suggest a strong correlation between the protective factors for strengthening and em-

Lynn McDonald was affiliated with Family Service, Madison, WI. Thomas V. Sayger is affiliated with the University of Memphis.

Address correspondence to: Lynn McDonald, Wisconsin Center for Education Research, The FAST Project, University of Wisconsin-Madison, 1025 West Johnson, Madison, WI 53706.

The authors want to acknowledge Family Service America, and K. Jones for their contributions and help with Figures 1 and 2. They also want to acknowledge J. DiPerna for his help with Figure 3. Acknowledgments to the dedicated FAST facilitators who collected the data.

The contents of this article are the sole responsibility of the authors and do not necessarily represent the official view of any of the funding agencies. The FAST Program is sponsored by Family Service, Madison, Wisconsin; the demonstration grant was funded by Center for Substance Abuse Prevention (CSAP) High Risk Youth Demonstration Grant #3699 from 1991 to 1996.

powering families, parent involvement in their child's schooling, and reports of child functioning, suggesting that as the parent's involvement increases, their child's functioning also improves. Unanticipated outcomes of the current implementation of the FAST program included the generalization of increased parent self-esteem to greater empowerment in community activities and the discovery of a high level of effectiveness of FAST parent graduates as program facilitators. *[Article copies available for a fee from The Haworth Document Delivery Service: 1-800-342-9678. E-mail address: getinfo@haworth.com]*

## INTRODUCTION

The Office of National Drug Control Policy (ONDCP) submitted a White Paper (August, 1993) identifying and reviewing the ten most promising substance abuse prevention programs. The White Paper concluded that effective prevention efforts need to address multiple domains. The multi-domain program identified by ONDCP which used a family-based approach, was the Families and Schools Together (FAST) program which had been developed by the senior author in 1988 (McDonald et al., 1991, 1997; McDonald, 1992, 1993). This manuscript uses the domain matrix approach developed by the Center for Substance Abuse Prevention (De Jong, 1995) to evaluate effects of this program on multiple domains.

A rare, fifteen year study on adolescent substance abuse (Shedler & Block, 1990) examined multiple early variables which significantly distinguished the eighteen year old alcohol abuser. The effect of a critical family predictor, the amount of positive bonding between mother and child at ages three, five, and seven is not impacted by educational prevention programs. Shedler and Block concluded that early intervention which addresses family processes and increases positive bonding is of significant importance.

The conceptual framework underlying the FAST program is that of building protective factors throughout several domains of the at-risk child's social ecology (Bronfrenbrenner, 1979; Garbarino, 1980). With the development of these protective factors, the child will be less likely to experience substance abuse, violence and delinquency, and school dropout. FAST's entry point for prevention/early intervention is the family, based on the assumption of the parents' love and concern for their child. The parent-child bond is seen as the primary influence in the child's ecology. It is through parental desire for their child to succeed in life that one can recruit resistant and alienated parents into voluntary participation in a substance abuse prevention program. The program builds multiple protective factors which strengthen the parent-child relationship and builds informal and formal social supports for the parents. This foundation of support empowers the parent so that s/he can succeed in being central to the prevention process for their own child. Protective factors in seven distinct domains (i.e., mother-child bond, parent to parent bond, cohesive family unit, parent self-help group, parent-school affiliation, parent to community agency connections, empowerment of parent/positive attitude) are built during the FAST program. Each of these factors is a positive bond simultaneously enhanced during the program through relationships within families, across families, between families and schools, and between families and community agency professionals. This paper will review these protective factors and the interventions developed to build these factors and report on the evaluation assessing the impact of the interventions.

## PROTECTIVE FACTORS AND INTERVENTIONS

### Protective Factor I: Mother-Child Bond

The positive, empathic, mutual bond between the mother and the child is correlated with many positive outcomes. Strategy for enhancing this bond is based on the clinical research of Kogan, Gordon, and Wimberger (1972) and Kogan (1978, 1980). Their protocol, which resulted in a positive mother-child bond and improved child functioning, involved observing and coaching mothers to follow their child's lead without bossing, teaching, or criticizing during fifteen minute one-to-one sessions. The FAST "Special Play" strategy is structured so that each week of the eight to ten week program, the group of twelve participating mothers (or primary caretakers) spend fifteen minutes of quality time with their at-risk child while trained facilitators observe, support, and coach the mother toward success. Homework assignments are made for mothers to continue this "special play" for fifteen minutes a day over the next two years.

### Protective Factor II: Intimate Support Network:
### Parent to Parent Bond

A marriage which is a healthy partnership is characterized by clear communication, effective conflict resolution, and freedom to express range of emotions. Such a parent-to-parent bond is correlated with many positive child outcomes (Minuchin, 1986) while chronic conflict is damaging for the child (Hetherington, 1989). For low income, depressed parents, having an intimate supportive adult with whom one can converse on a daily basis reduces the likelihood of the daily stresses of life being taken out on the child (Belle, 1980). The FAST program builds the support potential of a parenting team through strengthening marital bonds or bonds between two single parents. For fifteen minutes of each multi-family meeting, the parents pair up into teams of two and are requested to listen to each other review the hassles of the day. Instructions are to not give advice, interrupt, fix the problem, or change the subject, but rather give feedback showing that one is listening.

## *Protective Factor III: Cohesive Family Unit*

When families are strong and cohesive, trust one another, share emotions together, communicate openly, and resolve conflicts easily, they can survive many hardships (Lewis, Beavers, Gossett, & Phillips, 1976; Sayger, 1992). Family therapists suggest that families are dysfunctional if: (a) the parents are not in charge of the family; (b) the family cannot resolve conflict through communication; (c) there is low family cohesiveness and members are disengaged from one another (Alexander, 1973; Minuchin, 1979). A disengaged, conflicted, disorganized family is considered to be a causal factor to violence and delinquency, substance abuse, and school failure. There is growing evidence that systemic (i.e., family systems-centered) drug interventions are effective in helping family members with their addictions (Lewis, Piercy, Sprenkle, & Trepper, 1990).

Family Cohesion is considered the *central protective factor* in the FAST framework and is achieved by strengthening family communication and their ability to resolve conflict. The FAST parents are put in charge of their own family using several strategies: the collaborative team helps children serve a meal to their parents, parents are given instructions (rather than the children) and direct their child's actions, and staff support the parent in order to maximize their experience of success with their own children.

New behavioral interaction sequences are practiced in family units throughout each of the FAST program elements: (1) families sit together for one hour at a family table which they decorate with a family-constructed flag; (2) parents direct two, fun family games which specifically include communications exercises and adhere to the interactional rules for conflict resolution in the family (i.e., put parents in charge of their family, take turns speaking, listen to each family members' perspective, do not criticize) (Alexander & Parsons, 1973). One game involves acting out feelings, guessing the emotion, and talking about them in the family. The other game involves drawing something and talking about it within the family. The two exercises build positive, affectionate, sustaining familial bonds. Each of these exercises addresses family issues which have been shown to be correlated with adolescent substance abuse, alcohol-related aggression (Elkin, 1984) and juvenile delinquency (Kumpfer, 1994).

### Protective Factor IV: Parent Self-Help Support Group

Many researchers have studied support networks to identify the most salient components of an effective social network and the distinctions made between informal and formal support networks (Crnic, Greenberg, Robinson, & Ragozin, 1984). The mistake of many social interventions is the overreliance on formal networks (i.e., professionals and institutions) and the lack of respect for informal support networks (i.e., peers). Research shows that informal support networks are more reliable and constant over time and people feel more comfortable using them. The informal networks are more flexible and individuated to the specific needs of the family under stress, more culturally sensitive, and less expensive to society. The FAST Program builds informal support networks. The effective elements for recruiting families into voluntary participation in the multi-family program include: (1) home visits made by members of the collaborative team which includes a parent graduate of FAST; (2) training in recruitment language to include matching what the parent expresses as a concern about their child; (3) recruiting the whole family through a shared concern about the child; (4) removing obstacles for participation (e.g., transportation, child care); (5) providing both consistent and intermittent multiple incentives for participation; and (6) respite from the children in an adult-only discussion group.

### Protective Factor V: Parent-School Affiliation

Parent involvement in the school system is integral to the academic achievement and psychosocial functioning of the child and Stevenson and Baker (1987) noted that mothers' involvement in their children's school activities affects the children's school performance independent of maternal educational status. Historically, parents of at-risk children have experienced a strained and, many times, overwhelmingly negative relationship with their child's school. Few parents of at-risk children will report incidents of being notified by their child's school because of a positive event, even though many positive events may have occurred (McDonald, 1993). The FAST program addresses the parent-school affiliation by helping parents to become more actively involved in their child's school activities. Children and families are referred to FAST via school personnel, each FAST group includes parents with children from the same school, many FAST groups meet in their child's school, and school personnel act as support staff during the FAST program. These activities set the stage for an environment in which school personnel and families can share positive activities without judging, parents meet other parents with similar concerns and develop a supportive cohort, and many positive activities become associated with the school setting, thus opening the doors for mutually respectful, cooperative and friendly communication between parent and school.

### Protective Factor VI: Parent to Community Agency Connections

As with schools, community agencies can be perceived as the enemy. Friesen (1993) noted that family-centered services should: (1) be individualized and flexible with emphasis placed on the needs, values, and preferences of the families; (2) be administered by professionals who work collaboratively with families, in settings of the families' choice, sharing information, responsibility, and power; (3) be structured as true inter-professional collaboration involving coordinated planning, with family members as full members of the team; and (4) place resources into flexible, community-based alternatives. The empowerment of families means helping families and children gain accurate information, access to resources, respite care, coping skills for managing problems, and social supports (Johnson, 1993). The FAST program works to empower access to formal support networks. The program includes active participation from parent graduates of FAST, provides self-help activities, offers information on community services, assists with transportation and respite care, and allows for discussion of ways to cope with stressful life events. Professional staff attend all multi-family meetings in the role of a supportive, respectful person (i.e., without a professional agenda).

### Protective Factor VII: Empowerment of Parent/Positive Attitude

There is increasing support for the idea that successful parenting is correlated with high parental self-esteem, having a feeling of power within one's family unit, and a sense of self-efficacy within society (Gaudin et al., 1993). Change is dependent on experiential learning, which includes experiences of success in parenting, of talking about and sharing one's successes as a parent with other parents, of being respected as a parent, and of being efficacious with people from different walks of life in getting things done. Positive social feedback within daily ecology are essential for maintenance of positive parenting and contributes to the parent's personal feelings of empowerment (Febrarro, 1994). FAST works to build feelings of empowerment in parents. Program activities include: (a) respectful home visits made at the family's convenience to invite families to voluntarily participate in the program; (b) each family experiences winning the lottery; (c) using the principle of reciprocity (Dunst, Trivette, & Deal, 1988), the following week the family is expected to give back to the program (the winning family gets cash to cook the meal for the whole FAST group the next week); thus, each family is singled out in two positive interpersonal experiences; (d) personal achievement announcements are made to the whole FAST group at the end of each meeting in a large circle; and (e) facilitators are trained in role playing exercises on how to empower parents in micro-event transactions.

## Overall Intervention Goals

The main goals of the program are: (1) to enhance family functioning by strengthening the parent-child relationship and empowering parents as primary prevention agents for their own children; (2) to prevent the referred child from experiencing school failure by improving the child's performance and behavior in school, involving parents in the educational process, and increasing the family's positive feeling of affiliation with the school; (3) to prevent substance abuse by children and the family by increasing knowledge and awareness of substance abuse and its impact in child development, and by linking families to assessment and treatment services; and (4) to reduce stress experienced by parents and children in daily situations by developing an informal support system among parents of at-risk children and linking families to community resources and services. The evaluation of the program was designed to evaluate and provide feedback on process as well as to provide outcome data evaluating achievement of program goals.

## METHODOLOGY

### Evaluation Design

The design of the series of studies reported in this manuscript provides both process evaluation data and outcome evaluation data. The basic design of the FAST program implementation and assessment follows a pre- and post-FAST assessment following the 8-weekly multi-family group meetings. A subsequent 6-month follow-up assessment is completed on participants that have completed the 8-week FAST program. The third phase of the study is a two-year follow-up of all families that have graduated from the FAST program.

Phase I of the current study entails a pre-test comparison of FAST participants in Madison with published norms on the Revised Behavior Problem Checklist (RBPC) for clinical and normal child populations. FAST programs were conducted at 2 elementary and 2 middle schools during the Fall and Spring semesters of each academic year (N = 104 families) from 1991 to 1996.

Phase II of the current study entails a non-experimental pre-test, post-test design to determine any changes in child behavior and family cohesion over the course of the families' FAST program participation. The sample for this part of Phase II includes 52 families with middle school-aged children and 52 families with elementary-aged school children that participated in the FAST program during the 1992-1996 academic years. Additionally, a non-experimental pre-test, post-test, and six-month follow-up design was employed to determine short-term maintenance of changes in child behavior and family cohesion over the course of the FAST program and a brief follow-up period. The sample for this portion of Phase II includes 20 of the 52 families with middle school-aged children and 31 of the 52 families with elementary school-aged children that participated in Phase I of the current study. Analyses were conducted in a matched pairs design for participant families who had also completed both pre-test and post-test assessment protocols. Missing data, completion of the grant period, and inability to contact some families accounts for the reduction in matched data sets for Phase II.

Phase III of the current study entails a non-experimental assessment of FAST graduates at a point 2-years after their completion of the FAST program. A sample of 251 participants from 1991-1994 completed the assessment protocol which included a survey questionnaire, the RBPC, and Family Adaptability and Cohesion Evaluation Scale-III (FACES-III). This sample consists of FAST participants in Madison, Wisconsin and includes families who participated in FAST both prior to and during the CSAP-funded study. In fact, a component of the CSAP grant was to determine the long-term impact of the FAST program on all graduates. Thus, only some of the sample in Phase III of this current project were represented in Phase II.

Analyses of these data emphasized in particular the protective factors noted to impact parent-child relationships and family functioning. Correlations between six protective factors and the central protective factor of family cohesion were computed as was the correlation between family cohesion and child functioning.

### Demographics of Participants

The multi-family group programs reported here were conducted at two elementary schools and two middle schools in Madison, Wisconsin, twice a year for four consecutive years, as funded under CSAP. Each 8-10 week program cycle graduated an average of six families. The demographics of the 104 participating FAST families for whom both pre- and post-scores from parents were available include: Primarily single parent, female-headed families (95%); receiving public assistance (90%); 60% without a car; 40% without a telephone; maternal mean age = 30 years; 75% of mothers had a high school education; average number of children in the household was 2.5; and ethnicity was 71% African-American, 22% European-American, 4% Asian-American, and 3% Hispanic-American. Children participating in the study were 56% male, scoring as at-risk on the RBPC scales, and average age was 8 years in the elementary school and 12 years in the middle school programs.

## *Measures*

The assessment of the FAST program impact on the participating high risk youth and their families focused on three general factors: (1) the behaviors of the high risk youth reported in the classroom and at home; (2) the closeness or cohesiveness of the family; and (3) changes in parent behavior, empowerment, social support, and involvement in their child's schooling. Youth behaviors were assessed using the Revised Behavior Problem Checklist (RBPC; Quay & Peterson, 1987), which was completed by both teachers and parents on each child at three time points. Family cohesion was measured using the Cohesion subscale of the *Family Adaptability and Cohesion Evaluation Scale* (FACES-III; Olson, 1982, 1986). The Follow-up Questionnaire focused on the long-term impact upon parents of systematically building the seven protective factors. Each item of the Follow-up Questionnaire was scored using a linear scale to reflect the range of involvement enabling statistical analysis.

## *Control/Comparison Groups and Analyses of Findings*

One primary issue of conducting applied research with at-risk and disenfranchised populations is obtaining meaningful control or comparison groups. The current study contrasted the CSAP-FAST-Madison data (N = 104) with four comparison groups:
1. with Quay and Peterson's (1995) published norms of the RBPC (parents version) on clinical (n = 96) and normal populations (n = 566) for children ages 6-12 years and Madison FAST participants (n = 22 on teacher RBPC) with normal (n = 972) students on the published norms for the teacher's version of the RBPC. This comparison, shown in Figure 1, indicated that Madison FAST children (N = 104) were at risk, though not

at clinical levels, at the onset of the study and mapped progress over two years toward the normal range.

2. with Family Service America National FAST Data Bank group norms on the RBPC (parents [n = 516]; teachers [n = 579]; McDonald, 1995). These norms can be used by local sites for contrast and comparison (Figure 2) with the congregate of FAST children nationally.

3. with themselves over time. A sample of 52 elementary and 52 middle school participants completed pre-FAST and post-FAST assessments (Table 1). A subsample of 31 elementary and 20 middle school FAST participants completed matched sets of pre-, post-, and 6-month follow-up assessments and these data are presented in Table 2. These data provide a means of comparing with paired t-tests the within family change over time.

4. within the Madison school district. FAST facilitators attempted to contact all FAST parent graduates (since the program began in 1988) at a point 2 or more years after FAST graduation for follow-up interviews and the completion of an RBPC and FACES-III. School district files were used to determine the whereabouts of the children in school and about 40% of our FAST population had moved out of the district. Interviews were conducted during 1994, 1995, and 1996. The total number of assessments completed by parents on their FAST child was 251; the total number of interviews with parents on various impact questions was 191. The FAST parents who were interviewed reported a wide range of ongoing involvement with the FASTWORKS program, including 28% who reported having never attended a FASTWORKS event (Table 3). This variable level of participation enabled the researchers to correlate various responses made to the survey with the outcomes of family cohesion and child functioning. These relationships are presented in a figure with correlations and probability statistics (Figure 3). In addition, the average RBPC two-year follow-up data (n = 191) are presented in Figure 1 with the RBPC scores of pre-post 104 FAST children, with the Quay-Peterson published norms for 6-12 year olds (Quay & Peterson, 1995).

### RESULTS

As stated earlier, the design of this study involved three phases (1) comparison of FAST participants to published norms for normal and clinical populations, (2) pre- to post-test and pre-post-follow-up matched comparisons, and (3) two-year follow-up interviews and assessment of FAST graduates. The results will be presented and discussed for each Phase of the study.

FIGURE 1. Revised Behavior Problem Checklist (*Quay-Peterson*): Published Parent Scale Norms of 6-12 Year Old Children Contrasted with FAST Parent Scores, Pre and Post, and 2 Year* Follow-Up, Madison, WI

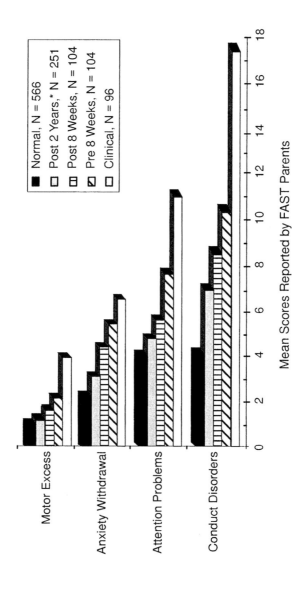

Mean Scores Reported by FAST Parents

*CSAP follow-up data from 251 Madison parents, 2-4 years after FAST graduation. This sample is non-overlapping with the 104 children referenced in the pre, post parts of the graph.

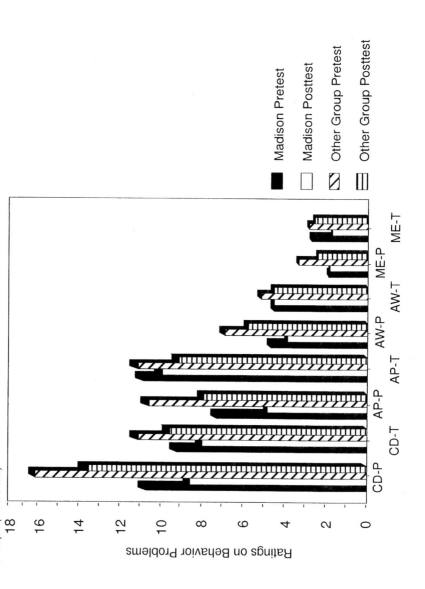

FIGURE 2. Revised Behavior Problem Checklist Results from CSAP Madison FAST Parents (P) and Teachers (T) Compared to Other FAST Groups (13 states)

TABLE 1. Results of Data Analyses on Pre- and Post-Assessments for Elementary (n = 52) and Middle School FAST Participants (n = 52) on the Revised Behavior Problem Checklist

| Subscale | Parent (n = 52) Pre | Post | t | p | Teacher (n = 22) Pre | Post | t | p |
|---|---|---|---|---|---|---|---|---|
| **Elementary School Program** | | | | | | | | |
| Conduct Disorder | 10.65 (8.80) | 8.58 (7.91) | 2.803 | .01 | 9.50 (10.61) | 8.14 (8.03) | 0.827 | n.s. |
| Socialized Aggression | 2.61 (3.46) | 1.94 (2.76) | 1.992 | .10 | 2.23 (4.02) | 1.86 (4.18) | 0.668 | n.s. |
| Attention Problems | 7.63 (6.97) | 5.50 (5.56) | 3.386 | .01 | 11.36 (7.46) | 10.45 (8.02) | 0.682 | n.s. |
| Anxiety/Withdrawal | 5.06 (4.72) | 4.35 (4.39) | 1.315 | n.s. | 4.55 (4.45) | 4.55 (4.61) | 0.001 | n.s. |
| Psychotic Behavior | 1.17 (1.66) | 0.85 (1.28) | 1.515 | n.s. | 1.14 (2.61) | 0.86 (2.05) | 1.031 | n.s. |
| Motor Excesses | 1.98 (2.19) | 1.72 (2.72) | 0.790 | n.s. | 2.77 (2.71) | 1.86 (2.17) | 1.815 | .10 |
| Total | 28.92 (21.94) | 23.26 (18.97) | 2.935 | .01 | 30.86 (24.35) | 27.91 (21.52) | 0.752 | n.s. |

TABLE 1 (continued)

| Subscale | Parent (n = 52) Pre | Post | t | p | Teacher (n = 22) Pre | Post | t | p |
|---|---|---|---|---|---|---|---|---|
| Middle School Program | | | | | | | | |
| Conduct Disorder | 10.35 (10.21) | 8.75 (8.33) | 1.664 | n.s. | | | | |
| Socialized Aggression | 5.23 (5.78) | 4.62 (5.14) | 0.872 | n.s. | | | | |
| Attention Problems | 7.85 (7.35) | 5.85 (5.95) | 2.084 | .05 | | | | |
| Anxiety/Withdrawal | 5.64 (4.98) | 4.45 (4.35) | 2.128 | .05 | | | | |
| Psychotic Behavior | 1.90 (2.21) | 1.33 (1.79) | 2.086 | .05 | | | | |
| Motor Excesses | 2.38 (2.61) | 1.77 (2.22) | 1.809 | .10 | | | | |
| Total | 33.12 (28.80) | 27.20 (24.25) | 1.971 | .10 | | | | |

Note: Standard deviations are in parentheses. RBPCs were not collected for the Middle School population as teachers are course specific and not in all day contact with students as in the elementary population.

TABLE 2. Results of Data Analyses on Pre-, Post-, and Follow-Up Assessments for Elementary School (n = 31) and Middle School (n = 20) FAST Participants on the Revised Behavior Problem Checklist

| Subscale | Parent (n = 31 Elementary, n = 20 Middle) | | | | | Teacher (n = 8 Elementary) | | | | |
|---|---|---|---|---|---|---|---|---|---|---|
| | Pre | Post | Fp | t | p | Pre | Post | Fp | t | p |
| **Elementary School Program** | | | | | | | | | | |
| Conduct Disorder | 9.65 (8.45) | 7.39 (7.40) | 6.84 (6.11) | 1.991 | .10 | 11.00 (10.72) | 9.25 (8.29) | 9.38 (8.78) | 1.188 | n.s. |
| Socialized Aggression | 2.29 (2.95) | 1.48 (2.01) | 1.29 (2.00) | 2.051 | .05 | 2.88 (4.29) | 1.62 (2.72) | 3.50 (3.93) | 1.122 | n.s. |
| Attention Problems | 7.29 (7.24) | 5.00 (5.32) | 5.03 (5.56) | 3.194 | .01 | 11.38 (5.80) | 10.25 (6.63) | 10.12 (5.59) | 1.318 | n.s. |
| Anxiety/Withdrawal | 4.87 (5.19) | 3.97 (4.19) | 3.52 (4.44) | 1.216 | n.s.** | 4.88 (3.72) | 3.75 (2.92) | 3.50 (3.42) | 1.136 | n.s. |
| Psychotic Behavior | 0.90 (1.69) | 0.48 (0.84) | 0.26 (0.51) | 1.453 | n.s.** | 1.50 (3.51) | 1.00 (2.45) | 1.75 (3.41) | 1.081 | n.s. |
| Motor Excess | 1.90 (2.23) | 1.19 (1.71) | 1.26 (1.81) | 2.484 | .02** | 3.50 (1.93) | 2.12 (2.10) | 2.12 (2.03) | 2.115 | .05 |
| Total | 26.75 (23.28) | 19.78 (17.59) | 18.34 (15.96) | 2.746 | .02 | 33.13 (20.13) | 28.50 (18.94) | 30.38 (17.46) | 1.518 | n.s. |

75

TABLE 2 (continued)

| Subscale | Parent (n = 31 Elementary, n = 20 Middle) | | | | | Pre | Teacher (n = 8 Elementary) | | | |
|---|---|---|---|---|---|---|---|---|---|---|
| | Pre | Post | Fp | t | p | | Post | Fp | t | p |
| **Middle School Program** | | | | | | | | | | |
| Conduct Disorder | 8.39 (10.31) | 7.39 (7.56) | 4.22 (6.12) | 1.716 | .10*** | | | | | |
| Socialized Aggression | 5.84 (6.51) | 4.15 (5.51) | 2.15 (3.94) | 1.576 | n.s.*** | | | | | |
| Attention Problems | 7.10 (6.53) | 5.60 (7.04) | 2.75 (3.03) | 1.133 | n.s.*** | | | | | |
| Anxiety/Withdrawal | 6.34 (5.34) | 4.66 (5.06) | 2.76 (2.79) | 1.435 | n.s.*** | | | | | |
| Psychotic Behavior | 1.65 (1.58) | 1.15 (1.64) | 0.45 (1.04) | 1.808 | .10* | | | | | |
| Motor Excess | 2.17 (2.57) | 1.83 (2.26) | 1.00 (1.94) | 1.106 | n.s. | | | | | |
| Total | 29.81 (23.68) | 23.19 (24.93) | 13.81 (17.38) | 1.735 | .10*** | | | | | |

Note: Standard deviations are listed in parentheses. Those levels of significance with no asterisks maintained significance at the levels reported. * There is no significant difference between Pre- and Post-Assessments. ** There is a significant difference between Pre- and Follow-up Assessments at the .10 level. *** There is a significant difference between Pre- and Follow-up Assessments at the .01 level.

TABLE 3. FASTWORKS Follow-Up Survey Responses of FAST Parent Graduates from FAST Programs in Madison Schools Two or More Years Post-FAST (N = 191)

| Protective Factor* | Percentage | Protective Factor | Percentage |
|---|---|---|---|
| **I: Mother-Child Bonding** | | **II. Intimate Support Network: Parent-Parent Bonding** | |
| How often do you do Special Play these days? | | A. Did you make friends? | |
| Daily | 16 | Yes | 86 |
| 2-3 Times/Week | 27 | No | 14 |
| Once/Week | 20 | | |
| 1-2 Times/Month | 22 | | |
| Rarely | 15 | | |
| | | B. How often do you keep in touch with FAST friends outside FAST-WORKS? | |
| **IV: Self-Help Support Group** | | Frequently | 14 |
| How often do you attend FASTWORKS meetings? | | Once in awhile | 45 |
| More than once/month | 21 | Rarely | 18 |
| Once/month | 16 | Never | 23 |
| Once every other month | 6 | | |
| Once every six months | 12 | | |
| Once/year | 17 | | |
| Never | 28 | | |

## TABLE 3 (continued)

| Protective Factor* | Percentage | | Protective Factor | Percentage |
|---|---|---|---|---|

### V: Parent-School Affiliation

A. Do you feel more like a partner with your child's school?

| | |
|---|---|
| Much more | 38 |
| Somewhat more | 47 |
| Somewhat less | 10 |
| Much less | 5 |

B. Do you think you are now more involved in your child's school than you were before starting FAST?

| | |
|---|---|
| Much More | 30 |
| Somewhat More | 42 |
| Not Any More | 28 |

### VII: Empowerment of Parent/Positive Attitude

A. How would you rate your level of self-esteem since FAST?

| | |
|---|---|
| Much Higher | 40 |
| Somewhat higher | 55 |
| Somewhat lower | 3 |
| Much lower | 2 |

B. Do you feel more powerful in helping your child?

| | |
|---|---|
| Much More | 45 |
| Somewhat More | 51 |
| Somewhat Less | 3 |
| Much Less | 1 |

### VI. Parent to Community Agency Connections

A. What are the activities in which you have been involved in the community since FAST?

| | |
|---|---|
| Counseling for self or children | 26 |
| AA/or Substance Abuse Treatment | 8 |
| Full-time Job | 30 |
| Part-time Job | 24 |
| Further Education | 44 |
| Volunteer Organizations | 14 |
| Community Center | 35 |
| Church | 32 |
| Parent-Teacher Organization | 17 |

*Protective Factor III: Cohesive Family Unit was measured by the FACES-III Cohesion scale. (See Figure 3.)

FIGURE 3. Protective Factors of FAST/FASTWORKS Program Correlated with Family Cohesion and Child Functioning

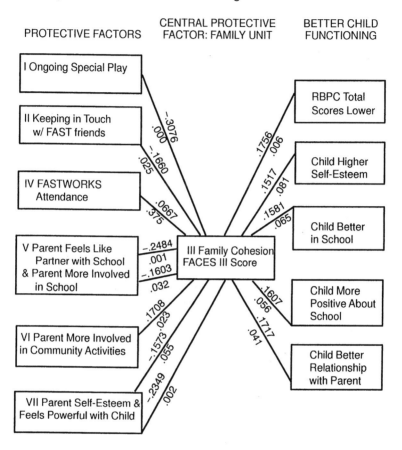

## Phase I

RBPC scores for the teacher-referred at-risk children, when compared to the published norms on the RBPC (Quay & Peterson, 1995) for clinical and normal children between the ages of 6 and 12 years show that prior to FAST, parents reported their children to score midway between clinical and normal children on the Conduct Disorder (CD), Attention Problems (AP), Anxiety/Withdrawal (AW), and Motor Excesses (ME) subscales (Figure 1). Teacher assessments also indicated scores consistent with those of at-risk children, with the exception of scores at clinical levels on the Attention Span (AS), a scale most correlated with school achievement.

## Phase II

Pre-post RBPC scores on 104 FAST children (n = 52 elementary, n = 52 middle school) showed statistically significant improvement on parent (P) reports on Conduct Disorder (t = 2.803, p = .01), Attention Problems (t = 3.386, p = .01), and Total Behavior (t = 2.935, p = .01) for the elementary school program and the Attention Problems (t = 2.084, p = .05), Anxiety-Withdrawal (t = 2.128, p = .05), and Psychotic Behavior (t = 2.086, p = .05) scales for the middle school program (see Table 1).

The number of available parent RBPC scores for pre-, post-, and six-month follow-up dropped off, thus decreasing the power of statistical tests. However, comparisons suggested that gains may be maintained over time (see Table 2). The FAST children were improving in their functioning in areas of Conduct Disorder (p = .10 for elementary, p = .01 for middle school), Anxiety-Withdrawal (p = .10 for elementary, p = .01 for middle school) and Attention Span (p = .01 for elementary, p = .01 for middle school), which are highly correlated respectively with juvenile delinquency, substance abuse, and school failure. Teacher (T) reports on the RBPC for elementary school children were significant on the Motor Excess scale (t = 2.115, p = .05).

Scores on the FACES-III Cohesion scale suggest that participation in the FAST program does increase family cohesion (t = − .2498, p = .02) from pre- (Mean = 38.28) to post- (Mean = 40.05) assessment for the elementary school group; differences for the middle school group were not statistically significant (Pre-Mean = 35.47, Post-Mean = 35.57, t = − 0.098, p > .05). The pre-, post-, and follow-up scores for cohesion for the elementary school group (n = 31) indicate a possible trend (Pre-Mean = 38.57, Post-Mean = 40.46, Follow-up Mean = 40.66, t = − 1.872, p = .10) toward significant change and maintenance; however, the middle school group (n = 20) shows maintenance of pre-test levels of family cohesion (Pre-Mean = 33.30, Post-Mean = 35.50, Follow-up Mean = 34.70, t = − 1.407, p > .05).

## Phase III

Two-year follow-up RBPC parent scores on an inclusive FAST sample in Madison, Wisconsin, of 251 children, suggested maintenance of change over time on relevant scores when these scores are compared to the pre-post data collected on 104 children. When compared to the RBPC published norms, these scores suggested that the children continue to move toward normal children's scores.

The follow-up surveys which were completed on 191 families indicated that despite 28% who never attended FASTWORKS, multiple changes were being reported by the parents on the seven protective factors (see Table 3). In order to better understand these data, a total activities score was developed for the parents. This was simply additive for the substance abuse treatment, family counseling, job, further education, PTA involvement, etc. When these scores were completed, only 7% of the population listed no new social involvement, 35% listed one, 25% listed two, 12% listed three, and 20% listed four or more. Then the multiple variables were entered into a multiple correlation matrix. This was the basis for developing the explanatory conceptual framework displayed in Figure 3. Each variable from the protective factors was entered onto the grid and the level of correlation and the probability that this was related to chance is listed for each variable.

Each of the protective factors (PF), with the exception of one (attendance at FASTWORKS meetings), was statistically significant to the central protective factor of family cohesion (as measured by the FACES-III) (i.e., PF-I [mother-child bond], r = −.3076, p = .000; PF-II [intimate social network], r = −.1660, p = .025; PF-V, [partner with school] r = −.2484, p = .001, [more involved with school] r = −.1603, p = .032; PF-VI [parent-community connections], r = .1708, p = .023, and PF-VII, [parent self-esteem] r = −.1573, p = .055, [powerful with child] r = −.2349, p = .002). The family cohesion score in turn was statistically significantly correlated with the child functioning as measured by the RBPC Total score (r = .1756, p = .006), the parent report of increased child self-esteem (r = .1517, p = .081), of child doing better in school (r = .1581, p = .065), of child feeling more positive about school (r = .1607, p = .056), and of child having a better relationship with the parent (r = .1717, p = .041). In addition, the FACES-III cohesion scale score for FAST parent graduates at the 2-year follow-up assessment (Mean = 38.68) was consistent with pre-FAST (Mean = 36.88) and post-FAST mean scores (Mean = 37.81).

Finally, two measures directly related to (1) the parent's increased knowledge about substance abuse and (2) whether the parent had gone into treatment were conducted. Eight percent of the surveyed sample reported that they had gone into treatment. Ninety-five percent of the parents reported having greatly or somewhat increased their knowledge about substance abuse. When the RBPC scores of the children of those parents who reported going into treatment were contrasted with the scores of the children whose parents did not report going into treatment were compared, with a t-test, there was a highly statistically significant difference (p = .013) between the two groups. The children of the substance abusing parents were by parent report on the RBPC nearly twice as problematic (RBPC Total Mean = 33.75, SD = 25.92) as the other children (RBPC Mean Total = 18.71, SD = 19.55).

## DISCUSSION

Evaluation of a community-based, school supported prevention program is a process, characterized by many adjustments. Substantial time must be committed to negotiations amongst collaborators and a general openness to critical inquiry and feedback must be nurtured. The process is facilitated when, as in this project, community agency professionals are "active" consumers of professional research and journals, and academic researchers are knowledgeable regarding clinical and community issues. Open lines of communication involving all staff and solicitating participant feedback set the stage for catching misunderstanding and other potential problems at early stages.

There was general resistance to quantitative research which was shared by the FAST practitioners and parents. Both groups agreed that reducing a person to a numerical score was in direct opposition to the values of FAST. Much of this initial resistance was overcome by requesting parent feedback on each questionnaire and having frequent discussions with FAST practitioners in which their concerns were listened to and respected. Additionally, evaluative data were shared with FAST staff along with interpretations of the findings and their implications for program development, while FAST practitioners were encouraged to ask questions, offer feedback, and suggest revisions. Parents expressed some discomfort and resistance to comparing their children to other children and noted that, contrary to the positive emphasis of FAST, items on many of the questionnaires tended to focus on problems or negative traits of their children. Attempts were made to assure parents that information was reported as group results, guidelines for confidentiality of information were closely followed, and that these instruments were only being used to establish general information on behaviors, interactions, and attitudes of participants.

Issues of attrition became a primary issue for long-term follow-up of FAST participants. These participants are characterized by high levels of mobility and the targeted schools were in very low income neighborhoods. Some staff turnover resulted in the loss of relationships and positive bonds between facilitators and FAST participant families. These bonds contributed to compliance with the assessment protocol and ease of tracking; with their loss, payments had to be instituted as incentives for participation in evaluation.

Several important unanticipated outcomes emerged which indicated areas requiring attention in future research studies. One outcome had to do with an informal experiment to determine the necessary qualifications for being a successful facilitator for the FAST program. Quantitative data was compared for groups facilitated by FAST parent graduates with that from groups facilitated by professionally trained individuals. The data were suggestive that an MSW was not necessary for facilitating effective FAST groups; the FAST parent graduates were as successful as the other more highly professionally trained facilitators in bringing about improvement in the behaviors of the at-risk children and cohesiveness in the families. Because of the underlying commitment of the FAST program to parent empowerment, this finding is of particular interest. It suggests that ultimately the FAST groups could routinely be facilitated by FAST parent graduates. This is a program that can empower parents to be their own child's prevention agent, and can empower some parents to run their own empowerment prevention program.

A second outcome requiring further study, had to do with the emergence of anecdotal data suggesting that empowerment of parents was taking place upon a broader spectrum than that measured by the evaluation. The FAST program identifies high risk youth and invites their families to participate in a multi-family, collaborative prevention program which has as its fundamental value that parents are the high risk child's primary prevention agent. In order to achieve this, FAST parents are provided informal and formal social supports which empower them in their parenting role. It was observed that these disenfranchised, poor, single mothers over time begin to act in empowered ways across other domains of functioning. The positive impact on the FAST parents' self-esteem of feeling effective and supported in their maternal role appears to generalize later into effective efforts toward self-sufficiency and, in some cases, community leadership and FAST-PAC (Parent Advisory Council) leadership.

Given the caveats about high attrition rates where there is no information available, and the lack of control groups as discussed above, any results must be considered with great caution. On the other hand, the FAST intervention is itself constructed to apply the results of some of the best experimental research available in the social sciences today. The goal here is not to discover something new, but to apply the already discovered effective strategies for "clinical" children with severe problems to the at-risk population of teacher-identified school children.

REFERENCES

Alexander, J. F. (1973). Defensive and supportive communications in normal and deviant families. *Journal of Consulting and Clinical Psychology, 40,* 223-231.

Alexander, J. F., & Parsons, B. V. (1973). Short-term behavioral intervention with delinquent families: Impact on family process and recidivism. *Journal of Abnormal Psychology, 81,* 219-225.

Belle, D. (1980). *Low income depressed mothers: Parent intervention.* Cambridge, MA: Harvard University Press.

Bronfrenbrenner, U. (1979). *The human development: Experiments by nature and design.* Cambridge, MA: Harvard University Press.

Crnic, K., Greenberg, M. T., Robinson, N. M., & Ragozin, A. S. (1984). Maternal stress and social support: Effects on the mother-infant relationship from birth to eighteen months. *American Journal of Orthopsychiatry, 54,* 224-255.

De Jong, J. A. (1995). An approach for high risk prevention research. *Drugs & Society, 8,* 125-138.

Dunst, C., Trivette, C., & Deal, A. (1988). *Enabling and empowering families: Principles and guidelines for practice.* Cambridge, MA: Brookline Books.

Elkin, M. (1984). *Families under the influence: Changing alcoholic patterns.* New York: W. W. Norton.

Febrarro, A. R. (1994). Single mothers at risk for child maltreatment: An appraisal of person-centered interventions and a call for emancipatory action. *Canadian Journal of Community Mental Health, 13,* 47-60.

Garbarino, J. (1980). *Adolescent development: An ecological perspective.* Columbus, OH: Charles E. Merrill.

Gaudin, J. M., Polansky, N. A., Kilpatrick, A., & Shilton, P. (1993). Loneliness, depression, stress, and social supports in neglectful families. *American Journal of Orthopsychiatry, 63,* 597-605.

Hetherington, E. M. (1989). Coping with family transitions: Winners, losers, and survivors. *Child Development, 60,* 1-14.

Johnson, H. C. (1993). Family issues and interventions. In H.C. Johnson (Ed.), *Child mental health in the 1990's: Curricula for graduate and undergraduate professional education.* Rockville, MD: US DHHS, 86-105.

Kogan, K. L. (1978). Help seeking mothers and their children. *Child Psychology and Human Development, 8,* 204-218.

Kogan, K. L. (1980). Interaction systems between preschool handicapped or developmentally delayed children and their parents. In T. M. Field, S. Goldberg, D. Stern, & A. M. Sostek (Eds.), *High-risk infants and children: Adult and peer interactions* (pp. 227-247). New York: Academic Press.

Kogan, K. L., Gordon, B. N., & Wimberger, H. C. (1972). Teaching mothers to alter interactions with their children: Implications for those who work with children and parents. *Childhood Education, 49,* 107-110.

Kumpfer, K. L. (1994). *Strengthening America's families: Promising parenting and family strategies for delinquency prevention: User's guide.* Office of Juvenile Justice and Delinquency Prevention, US Department of Justice. Silver Spring, MD: Aspen Systems.

Lewis, J. M., Beavers, W. R., Gossett, J. T., & Phillips, V. A. (1976). *No single thread: Psychological health in family systems.* New York: Brunner/Mazel.

Lewis, R. A., Piercy, F. P., Sprenkle, D. H., & Trepper, T. S. (1990). Family-based interventions for helping drug abusing adolescents. *Journal of Adolescent Research, 5,* 82-95.

McDonald, L. (1992). *Families and schools together (FAST): Orientation manual and a program workbook.* Madison, WI: Family Service, Inc.

McDonald, L. (1993). *Families and schools together: Final report for OHD/ACF/ DHHS Grant #90-PD-165.* Madison, WI: Family Service, Inc.

McDonald, L. (1995). *FAST national evaluation report.* Milwaukee: Family Service America.

McDonald L., Billingham S., Conrad P., Morgan A., O, N., & Payton, E. (1997). Family and schools together (FAST); Integrating community development with clinical strategy. *Families in Society,* pp. 140-155 (March/April).

McDonald, L., Coe-Braddish, D., Billingham, S., Dibble, N., & Rice, C. (1991). Families and Schools Together: An innovative substance abuse prevention program. *Social Work in Education, 13,* 118-128.

Minuchin, S. (1979). *Families and family therapy.* Cambridge, MA: Harvard University.

Minuchin, S. (1986). *Family kaleidoscope.* Cambridge, MA: Harvard University Press.

Office of National Drug Control Policy. (1993). *Review of drug prevention programs: A White House paper.* Washington, D.C.

Office of Substance Abuse Prevention. (1990). *Ecology of alcohol and other drug use: Helping black high risk youth.* Rockville, MD: US Department of Health and Human Services, US Government Printing Office.

Olson, D. H., (1986). Circumplex model VII: Validation studies and FACES III. *Family Process, 25,* 337-351.

Quay, H. C., & Peterson, D. R. (1987). *Manual for the revised behavior problem checklist.* Coral Gables, FL: University of Miami, Department of Psychology.

Quay, H. C., & Peterson, D. R. (1995). *Manual for the revised behavior problem checklist.* Coral Gables, FL: University of Miami, Department of Psychology.

Sayger, T. V. (1996). Creating resilient children and empowering families using a multifamily group process. *Journal for Specialists in Group Work, 21,* 81-89.

Shedler, J., & Block, J. (1990). Adolescent drug use and psychological health: A longitudinal inquiry. *American Psychologist, 45,* 612-630.

Stevenson, D.L. & Baker, D.P. (1987). The family-school relation and the children's school performance. *Child Development, 58,* 1348-1357.

# Effectiveness
# of the Logan Square Prevention Project:
# Interim Results

Mark D. Godley, PhD
Rick Velasquez, MSW

SUMMARY. Even though substance abuse prevention programs have been studied for more than two decades, outcome studies of programs focused on inner-city youth are rare. Communities with dense populations, low socio-economic conditions and a high degree of neighborhood disorganization are especially vulnerable to high rates of adolescent substance abuse. The goal of this study was to organize a coalition of neighborhood agencies to provide a comprehensive array of school and community-based prevention services to reduce substance use and gang involvement among inner-city Latino

---

Mark D. Godley is affiliated with Chestnut Health Systems, Inc., and Rick Velasquez is affiliated with Youth Outreach Services, Inc.

Address correspondence to: Mark Godley, Chestnut Health Systems, 720 West Chestnut, Bloomington, IL 61701.

The authors thank Sharon Zahorodnyj and Thurman Byrd of the Illinois Department of Alcoholism and Substance Abuse for administrative support, Renee Hoewing-Roberson and Michelle Pillen for data analysis and test construction, and Susan Godley for her comments on an earlier draft. Appreciation is extended to Connie Schwartz for assistance with manuscript preparation.

This project was funded by the United States Center for Substance Abuse Prevention, Grant 5 H86 SP02884-04 to the Illinois Department of Alcoholism and Substance Abuse. The contents of this article are the sole responsibility of the authors and do not necessarily represent the official views of the funding agency.

[Haworth co-indexing entry note]: "Effectiveness of the Logan Square Prevention Project: Interim Results." Godley, Mark D., and Rick Velasquez. Co-published simultaneously in *Drugs & Society* (The Haworth Press, Inc.) Vol. 12, No. 1/2, 1998, pp. 87-103; and: *Substance Abuse Prevention in Multicultural Communities* (ed: Jeanette Valentine, Judith A. De Jong, and Nancy J. Kennedy) The Haworth Press, Inc., 1998, pp. 87-103. Single or multiple copies of this article are available for a fee from The Haworth Document Delivery Service [1-800-342-9678, 9:00 a.m. - 5:00 p.m. (EST). E-mail address: getinfo@haworth.com].

*87*

youth. An institutional cycles quasi-experimental design was used to evaluate the effectiveness of this project. Participants were 651 pretest cohort students and 667 posttest cohort students attending grades 5-8 in two Chicago elementary schools. The cohorts were from 75-79 percent Latino and from 16-18 percent African American.

Interim results supporting project goals showed that gang involvement was significantly lower among the posttest cohort compared to the pretest cohort. Statistical trends were found for decreased substance use and academic enhancement outcomes. A secondary analysis of predictors of youth at higher vs. lower risk for substance abuse problems was conducted: This revealed that gang involvement was the strongest predictor of substance abuse risk, followed by grade in school, perceived closeness to gangs, perceived closeness to family, lower grades, and gender. Future evaluation work on this project will assess the effectiveness of two additional posttest cohorts and establish the relationship between type and amount of services received and attained outcomes. *[Article copies available for a fee from The Haworth Document Delivery Service: 1-800-342-9678. E-mail address: getinfo@haworth.com]*

## INTRODUCTION

Substance use and abuse among adolescents continues to be a major problem in the United States. Survey research points to recent increases in drug use by youth after a relatively long period of declining usage (Johnston, 1994). Recent research has identified several risk factors that predispose youth to substance abuse. In their review of the literature on risk factors for adolescent substance abuse, Hawkins, Catalano, and Miller (1992) found 17 conditions that placed youth at risk for developing substance abuse problems. These risk factors can be divided into community risk conditions, family, and individual risk factors. Hence, community norms that promote substance use such as police tolerance of public intoxication or open-air drug sales normalize expectations for drug use in a given community. Early initiation of alcohol or other drug use (before age 14) has been associated with problem drug use and represents an individual risk factor. Additional risk factors promoting alcohol and other drug use by youth include family management problems (Patterson & Dishion, 1985), high availability/easy access to alcohol or other drugs (Maddahian, Newcomb, & Bentler, 1988), poor academic performance, and antisocial behavior such as gang involvement (Hawkins, Catalano, and Miller, 1992).

Communities with dense populations, low socio-economic conditions and a high degree of neighborhood disorganization are especially vulnerable to high rates of adolescent substance abuse (Murray, Richards, Luepker, & Johnson, 1987; Sampson, 1985). Such communities are often the inner-city of major metropolitan areas. Epstein, Botvin, Diaz, and Schinke (1995) studied inner-city minority youth to examine what influenced their intention to use or actual use of alcohol. The strongest influencers identified in this research included family structure (single vs. two-parent family), the quality of the parent-child relationship, and parents' attitudes toward alcohol use and drunkenness. The prevalence of drinking among friends and peers, drinking status of the person they most admired, and knowledge of health-related information about alcohol use were all predictors of alcohol use.

Prevention programs designed to reduce youth vulnerability to environmental pressures promoting substance use and increase their coping and resistance skills are needed. Programs that increase youth self-esteem and self-confidence, and improve their decision-making while teaching specific refusal skills relative to social influences to use substances have been recommended (Schinke, Botvin, and Orlandi, 1991). Other researchers suggest that a salient design feature of successful prevention interventions is to extend programming into the community to reinforce or supplement school-based efforts (Pentz, MacKinnon, Flay, Hansen, Wang, and Johnson, 1989).

While substance abuse prevention programs have been studied for more than two decades, outcome studies of programs focused on inner-city minority youth have been relatively rare. In an effort to stimulate prevention services and evaluate their effectiveness in such communities, the United States Center for Substance Abuse Prevention (CSAP) developed a special demonstration grant program for high-risk youth. The majority of these projects are funded in urban communities where youth are subject to multiple risk conditions. This report focuses on one such program, located in a Latino neighborhood known as Logan Square–an inner-city neighborhood in Chicago. The goal of the Logan Square Prevention (LSP) project was to organize a coalition of neighborhood agencies to provide a comprehensive array of school and community-based prevention services in order to reduce alcohol and other drug use and gang involvement among inner city Latino youth. Several assumptions underlie the program model:

- Involving several neighborhood agencies in a comprehensive prevention plan will be more effective than a single agency providing services to high-risk youth through a single medium (e.g., schools)

- Providing higher service dosages for youth by serving them over several years and involving multiple agencies will be more effective than short-term intervention
- Providing culturally-specific programming will be more effective than programs developed for white, middle-class adolescents
- Providing an intervention that addresses salient risk conditions such as gang involvement, academic failure, and unstructured free time will be most effective in reducing alcohol and other drug abuse.

Results reported here are based on the first three years of a five-year demonstration project.

## *METHOD*

### *Target Population and Research Design*

The LSP project targeted all students in the fifth through eighth grades at two elementary schools in the Logan Square neighborhood. While the intervention was multifaceted and included many elements offered outside of the schools, measurement occurred annually in the schools. An institutional cycles quasi-experimental research design (Cook and Campbell, 1979) was employed for this study. This design is used for research conditions where participants such as students are organized by age and grade, thus reducing unwanted variability in maturation.

An important feature of the research design was the longitudinal nature of the study. Because the project was funded for five years, outcome data can be analyzed by grade cohort. For example, project success would be supported if, by the end of year three, grade cohorts with more than one year of services performed better than those with less than one year of service. Specifically the fifth, sixth, seventh, and eighth grade classes from the 1993 academic year were tested against 1992 fifth, sixth, seventh, and eighth grade classes.

### *Intervention*

This project is the result of concerned local representatives from church, law enforcement, education, and local service organizations who were convened by the Logan Square Neighborhood Association's Crime Committee in 1989 to address the complex task of alcohol and drug abuse prevention in the community. Recommendations from this group followed research findings suggesting that the most effective way to work with youth who exhibit multiple risk factors is to provide them with a comprehensive and coordinated range of programs within a network of services (Bry, 1983). Accordingly, a service consortium consisting of a lead agency and seven community-based organizations located in or near Logan Square received CSAP funding in 1991. The project was led by a youth service agency with over 25 years of experience which includes the management of large federal grants. This organization served as the lead agency and was responsible for negotiating, supervising, and monitoring the performance and subcontractual arrangements for the seven consortium agencies. Participating agencies included:

1. Eight churches from different denominations were organized under a lead church. The churches served as neighborhood drop-in centers where project youth could participate in small group after-school programs including recreational activities, tutoring, life-skills training, substance abuse education, field trips, cultural awareness programs, and counseling.
2. The local district office of the Chicago Police Department was contracted to conduct annual gang prevention seminars in the target schools, organize large scale recreational/sporting events at one of the target schools (e.g., Annual School Olympics Program), and organize neighborhood groups such as block clubs and school parent groups to reduce threats of gang violence.
3/4. Two Boys and Girls Clubs located near each participating school provided school-based life-skills curriculum (SMART Moves) and engaged target youth in special after-school/summer program activities at the clubs.
5. A small Latino youth service organization provided bilingual and bicultural in-school substance abuse prevention and life-skills education to 40-50 Spanish-speaking students annually.
6. One of the initial Chicago settlement houses was funded to provide in-school and after-school counseling services to youth and their families which identified family or behavioral problems using trained bilingual/bicultural social workers and graduate students.
7. A Latino drug abuse treatment and prevention agency received funds to educate and provide support services to parents of the participating students.

### Measures

*Model Implementation.* Implementation of the model was measured in two ways. First, since a major goal of the project was to organize the consortium members into a cohesive group that avoided duplicative services by collaborating with one another, a network analysis measure was used to assess the extent of cooperative networking by consortium members. Second, services delivered by the church/social service agencies were tracked by individual target population participants through an automated service tracking system. This system was to provide agency staff with feedback as to the adequacy of implementation and target population penetration.

Several variables examining the different ways in which the consortium agencies interacted with each other were measured at monthly intervals. The main variables of interest included information exchange (e.g., letters, face-to-face discussions, phone calls, interagency committee meetings) and resource exchange (e.g., staff training sessions, joint staff meetings, community events). These categories were adapted from Van de Ven and Ferry's (1980) organizational psychology framework to more appropriately describe the Logan Square consortium. All networking variables were measured in terms of the number of activities initiated by each of the consortium agencies over a month's time period. In addition to noting the "sender" or initiator of each type of interaction, the "receiver" of each was also recorded. Monthly networking data sheets were submitted by consortium agency staff to tally the various types of interactions they initiated with other consortium members.

The automated service tracking system was developed using relational database software. Databases were developed for participant enrollment and prevention service tracking. Service dimensions included: (a) drug education; (b) outreach; (c) recreation; (d) educational enhancement; (e) life-skills training; (f) group counseling; (g) home visits; (h) individual counseling; (i) cultural education; (j) parent education; and (k) other. A service "ticket" was used to record service episodes to one or more youth. Services to individual youth were automatically summarized through the data base software.

*Acculturation Variable.* Previous research has suggested that Latinos, to the extent that they are acculturated (i.e., become a part of the dominant culture), experience higher levels of substance abuse. A measure of acculturation was constructed to assess the extent to which this variable functioned to protect Latino youth from substance abuse and gang involvement. Development of this measure was based on Olmedo's (1979) review of acculturation scales.

*Effectiveness.* The intervention focused on providing structured social and recreational activities, academic tutoring, substance abuse education for youth and parents and anti-violence and gang education. Accordingly, the major outcomes of interest were academic performance, gang involvement, family closeness vs. gang closeness, and alcohol, tobacco, and other drug use.

A survey was constructed to measure the above outcomes plus acculturation. Throughout its development, the survey was designed to be culturally appropriate for the Latino target population by seeking input, review, and comment from key project stakeholders. To ensure standardized administration, a protocol was developed which outlined administration instructions. Additionally, a two hour training session was provided to orient those conducting the survey.

The resultant survey had ten scales: (a) parent/family acculturation; (b) self/peer language acculturation; (c) customs acculturation; (d) food/popular culture acculturation; (e) past month substance use; (f) past year substance use; (g) lifetime substance use; (h) gang involvement; (i) family closeness; and (j) gang closeness. The survey also included a demographic section and a question regarding grades on respondent's last report card.

Degree of acculturation was defined as the degree to which an individual had adopted characteristics of the dominant culture. The Latino youth acculturation scale consisted of 18 items asking about the language use of respondent, their parents, and their peers; the type of television programs watched, and type of music listened to by the individual respondent and the respondent's family. Higher scores denoted higher levels of acculturation. In addition, this information was assessed for Puerto Ricans, Mexican-Americans, and all other Latino groups.

Substance use was measured through three sets of ten questions each. The first set asked the respondent the number of times they used each of eight different substances over their entire lifetime. Questions regarding use of the same ten substances, but over time frames for the past year and past month made up the other two sets of questions. Three indexes were created for lifetime, past year, and past month use by summing the responses for the ten items within each set. Higher scores denote greater substance use.

The degree of gang involvement was assessed through a scale that consisted of 17 items asking about the respondent's participation in gang-related activities. The questions ranged from relatively superficial and tangential involvement (e.g., "Was there gang activity in your neighborhood?" and "Did you wear gang colors?") to more serious involvement (e.g., " Did you hurt a gang member in a fight?" and "Did you sell drugs for a gang?"). The scale was created by summing the number of "yes" responses with higher scores denoting greater involvement.

The Gang Closeness and Family Closeness Scales were in the form of two parallel sets of five questions each, for example, "I felt I could be myself around family members" and "I felt I could be myself around gang members." Higher scores on these scales denote greater feelings of closeness.

Demographic questions were asked concerning gender; ethnic identification of self, parent, and friends; birthplace and country of residence of self and parents; and grades on last report card.

## Data Analysis

*Network Analysis.* Descriptive network analyses were computed to assess the degree of coordination between the agencies over time. The analyses calculated the intensity of network interactions which is reflective of the strength of the network (how invested each agency is in the interorganizational relationship). This value was computed by examining the proportion of each agency's interactions compared to the output of the entire network. Measures of centrality/decentralization, or the degree to which each agency participated equally were calculated to determine changes over time on this dimension.

*Project Effectiveness.* The focus of statistical analyses has varied from year to year during the survey. After the first administration in October, 1991, interest was centered on validation of the individual scales and description of the sample in terms of baseline characteristics. The second administration (May, 1992) allowed for preliminary examination of change in the outcome measures, however implementation of program services was still relatively new and erratic. Therefore, no program effects were predicted at this point. The primary focus of this report is on the third administration which occurred in May, 1993 (the third year of the project) and after one-and-a-half years of program implementation. Students in grades 5-8 surveyed in May, 1993, served as the treated group (referred to as the "posttest cohort") while students from the same grades in May, 1992, served as the minimally-exposed comparison group (the "pretest cohort").

Statistical techniques used to analyze the survey data included principal components analysis, Cronbach's alpha, and analysis of variance for validity and reliability testing. A three-way analysis of variance model was used to analyze project effectiveness. Model factors were grade of participants (grades 5-8), school (two project schools), and group (pretest and posttest cohort). All significant omnibus tests were followed by Tukey-Kramer post hocs. Finally, stepwise discriminant function analysis was used to examine the differences between higher and lower risk youth.

## RESULTS

### Sample Demographics and Attrition

Eligible participants for the LSP project were 651 and 667 fifth through eighth grade students at two elementary schools for the pretest and posttest cohorts, respectively. Table 1 displays demographic characteristics for each cohort group. There were no significant differences between survey cohort groups on the reported demographic variables. Usable surveys for the project effectiveness analyses represented 90 percent for the pretest cohort (May, 1992) and 91 percent for the posttest cohort (May, 1993).

### Network Analysis

The average number of information exchanges rose steadily from fewer than 10 per agency each month to an average of 20 per agency at the time of the third survey administration. Similarly, resource exchanges increased from an average of two per agency in June of 1991 to 15 per agency each month by March, 1993. Network centrality for information exchanges, a measure of the degree to which an agency (or cluster of agencies) dominates a network, decreased from .79 to .51. The network centrality coefficient for resource exchanges dropped from a high of 1.0 in the initial months of the project to .63 at the time of the third survey. These findings indicate that the network members, over time, began to exchange information and resources to a more equal degree.

### Implementation

Because the service tracking system was new and required extensive documentation of services, the reliability of the system was suspect during this initial year of training and implementation. Specifically, the project leadership suspected that under-reporting of services would significantly underestimate the hours of services provided to participants. Since under-reporting should have been randomly distributed through the sample, a decision was made to look at lower- vs. higher-risk youth to determine if the consortium was reaching those in greatest need.

Analyses were performed comparing the amount of services received by youth considered to be at higher risk due to their higher levels of gang involvement or substance use compared to youths with lower gang involvement and substance use. These tests gave an indication of whether services were being received by participants in greatest need. Youth with scores of four or greater on the gang involvement scale were compared

TABLE 1. 1992 Pre-Test Survey Respondents vs. 1993 Post-Test Survey Respondents

| Demographic Characteristic | Pretest Cohort *n = 651* | Posttest Cohort *n = 667* |
|---|---|---|
| Grade | % | % |
| 5 | 24 | 24 |
| 6 | 28 | 28 |
| 7 | 24 | 24 |
| 8 | 24 | 24 |
| Gender | | |
| Male | 47 | 44 |
| Female | 53 | 56 |
| Ethnicity | | |
| Puerto Rican | 39 | 33 |
| Mexican-American | 28 | 27 |
| Other Latinos | 13 | 15 |
| African-American | 16 | 18 |
| Caucasian | 2 | 2 |
| Unknown | 2 | 5 |
| Generation | | |
| First | 33 | 29 |
| Second | 36 | 38 |
| Third | 31 | 33 |

with those scoring less than four in terms of hours of programming aimed at reduction of gang involvement. Those reporting high gang involvement received significantly more gang-related prevention programming relative to those youths reporting low gang involvement ($F[1,527] = 4.72$, $p = .030$). There was a tendency for those reporting high past year substance use (scores of three or higher on 14 point scale) to receive more drug education and life-skills programming compared to those youths reporting low past year substance use ($F[1,533] = 2.00$, $p = .084$). Finally, with regard to educational enhancement services, youths reporting grades of

C's or lower tended to receive more tutoring than did youths reporting grades of A's or B's ($F[1,522] = 1.94, p = .163$).

### Validity and Reliability of Survey

Principal components analysis of the acculturation scale confirmed four factors. The first labeled Family/Parental Acculturation included music listened to with the family, and dances and stories the family knows, in addition to items pertaining to parental language usage. The second factor, Self/Peer Language included items about respondent's language usage and that of their friends. The third factor, labeled customs was comprised of activities in which the respondent participated outside of the family in terms of music, stories, and holidays. The final factor of Food/Popular Culture included items relating to the type of food preferred when alone and when with the family. Item analysis of these subscales yielded Cronbach's alphas of .95, .89, .81, and .75 for Family/Parental Acculturation, Self/Peer Language, Customs, and Food/Popular Culture, respectively. The acculturation scales confirmed that first and second generation youth were significantly less acculturated than third generation youth on the Family/Parental Acculturation scale. For both the Self/Peer Language and Food/Popular Culture subscales first generation youth were significantly less acculturated than second generation, who were themselves less acculturated than third generation youth. Furthermore, Mexican American youth were less acculturated than Puerto Ricans and other Latino groups.

The gang involvement scale was also subjected to a principal components analysis which confirmed unidimensionality of the scale. Item analysis revealed that two items contributed little to the scale and were, therefore, dropped. The resultant Cronbach's alpha of the shortened, 15-item scale was .83. Predictably, the gang involvement scale was significantly higher for eighth graders relative to fifth graders, and boys were significantly more involved with gangs than were girls. Students who indicated mostly F's on their last report card were significantly more gang involved than "A" and "B" students and "C" students were significantly more involved than "B" students.

Both the closeness to gangs and closeness to family scales were unidimensional as intended. Cronbach's alphas were .82 and .68 respectively. The Attitude Toward School Scale yielded a Cronbach's alpha of .75. Youths who said they felt close to gangs and youths who said they didn't feel close to their families were both significantly more gang involved than youths who did not feel close to gangs and youths who felt close to their families.

With regard to lifetime substance use, seventh graders reported significantly higher use than fifth graders, and boys reported significantly more use than girls. Youth who were "D" or "F" students reported significantly higher use than either "A" or "B" students and "C" students reported significantly more substance use than did "B" students. Comparisons of substance use by seventh- and eighth-grade respondents in the LSP project with Latino respondents to the Illinois Youth Survey conducted in 1990 (Barrett and Senay, 1990) revealed higher prevalence of substance use for almost every drug surveyed. Though statistical comparisons were not possible, the LSP sample showed particularly higher prevalence of inhalant use.

### Project Effectiveness

Analysis of interim project effectiveness was conducted by comparing the posttest cohort (treated group from year 3) with the pretest cohort (minimally exposed group from year 2). Surveys one and two were conducted in the same academic year, while survey three was conducted one year after survey two. Analysis of variance for grade cohorts was used to assess project effectiveness between survey two (pretest cohort) and survey three (posttest cohort). For these analyses, youth at each individual grade level were compared against youth who were in the same grade in the previous academic year. Salient findings from this analysis are reported below.

With regard to past year substance use, the posttest cohort reported less use than the pretest cohort ($F[1,1096] = 2.44$, $p = .118$). As expected, a significant main effect of grade level was also found ($F[3,1096] = 19.22, p = .000$) with post hocs revealing that both seventh and eighth graders reported significantly greater substance use in the last year than did either fifth or sixth graders (see Figure 1). Gang involvement was significantly less by the posttest cohort relative to the pretest cohort ($F[1,1092] = 3.98$, $p = .046$) (see Figure 2). The expected main effect of grade level was also confirmed ($F[3,1092] = 69.70$, $p = .000$). Specifically, post hoc tests showed eighth graders were significantly more gang involved than were fifth graders. Relatedly, there was a tendency for the posttest cohort of fifth and sixth graders to feel less close to gangs than the pretest cohort, but the decrease for the pretest and posttest cohorts of seventh and eighth graders was marginal. Overall the effect produced a statistical trend ($F[3,1099] = 2.05, p = .105$). In terms of academic grades, a tendency was found for the pretest cohort to report higher grades than the posttest cohort at one of the schools, and for the posttest cohort to report higher grades than the pretest cohort at the other school ($F[1,1053] = 2.55; p = .110$) (see Figure 3).

FIGURE 1. Change in Past Year Substance Use Index by Grade

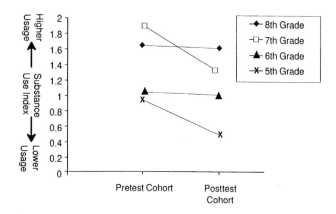

FIGURE 2. Change in Gang Involvement Scale by Grade

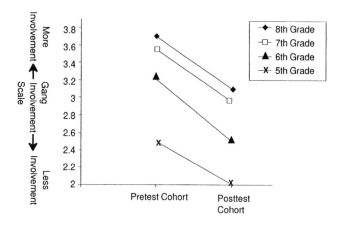

## Secondary Analysis

To examine differences between relatively higher-risk and lower-risk youth, stepwise discriminant function analysis was performed to assess the prediction of membership in the posttest cohort youth with past year substance use index scores of three or greater (higher risk) and those with scores of less than three (lower risk). Predictor variables included grade level in school, self-reported grades, gender, gang involvement, closeness to gangs, closeness to family, acculturation, and school attachment. Entry

FIGURE 3. Change in Grade Point Average by School

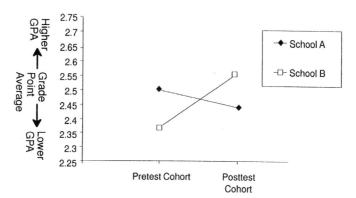

criteria of .05 probability of $F$-to-enter and .10 of $F$-to-remove were used. Entering the stepwise analysis first with an $F$-to-enter of 144.13 was gang involvement with higher-risk youth more gang involved than lower-risk youth. Second to enter was grade level in school ($F$-to-enter = 10.64) with higher risk youth being older. Higher-risk youth also felt closer to gangs (3rd step, $F$-to-enter = 5.11). Fourth to enter the stepwise analysis was closeness to family with higher-risk youth feeling less close than lower-risk youth ($F$-to-enter = 4.97). Entering at the fifth step was self-reported grades with higher-risk youth reporting lower grades ($F$-to-enter = 5.80) and gender entered at the sixth step ($F$-to-enter = 5.55) with higher-risk youth more likely to be male than lower-risk youth. Overall, the resulting equation correctly predicted 82 percent of the cases as either "high" or "low" risk for alcohol and other drug use.

### DISCUSSION

Evaluation of the LSP Project demonstrated that the consortium of prevention service providers substantially increased its degree of cooperation and collaboration, and that over time the network has become less dependent on the lead agency for information and resources and more decentralized or interdependent. Implementation data further suggests that the consortium was reaching those youth in greatest need of services to prevent academic failure, gang involvement, and substance abuse.

Outcome evidence from the quasi-experimental design suggests interim program effectiveness in reducing gang involvement for the posttest cohort. Gang involvement items that contributed to this effect were: (a) a 17 percent reduction in gang membership; (b) a 33 percent reduction in fights representing a gang; (c) a 32 percent reduction in carrying a weapon; (d) a 22 percent reduction in selling drugs for a gang; and (e) a 59 percent reduction in youth reporting they were part of the leadership of a gang. These results were also supported by the posttest cohort reporting less closeness to gangs than the pretest cohort.

Although the analysis of grade point average was not significant, the statistical trend toward an interaction of school by cohort group was interesting. Results of this analysis indicated that grades at one school decreased while grades at the other improved. Additional analysis of the service data showed that the school with improved posttest grades reached 26 percent of the students for academic enhancement services while the school with declining grades reached only 8.2 percent of the students.

While there was no significant change in the number of new alcohol and other drug users, there was a trend toward decreased alcohol and other drug use by the posttest cohort. The decline for Logan Square youth in past year alcohol and other drug use was primarily due to decreases in alcohol (44% to 40%), tobacco use (23% to 20%) and inhalant use (21% to 16%). Conversely, marijuana use increased from 6 percent to 10 percent of the posttest cohort.

Even more important than age (a strong predictor of increased usage of substance for school-aged youth) was gang involvement. This surprising finding, combined with the fact that the project achieved significant reductions in gang involvement, suggests that the LSP project may be making progress in accomplishing reductions in new and current substance use.

Despite the positive interim findings for this project, there are several limitations restricting the interpretation of these data. First, the research design does not rule out all alternative rival explanations to the findings. For example, it is possible that gang activity was generally declining for the Logan Square area or that the posttest cohort was, in some unmeasured way, at substantially less risk than the pretest cohort. An additional limitation of this study was the inability to conduct dose-response analyses to determine whether youth with higher levels of prevention services demonstrated less substance abuse or gang involvement than those with lower levels of services. Since the service tracking system was still relatively new and involved 14 different service function definitions, providers were not yet reliably coding all service data. Hence, analyses of services were limited to assessing the extent to which higher-risk youth versus lower risk youth received services.

One surprising finding, not taken into account in the initial selection of the target schools, was that both schools have high student mobility each year (50% and 37% for the two participating schools). High student mobility causes two major problems. First, the opportunity for both intensive and extensive service exposure for participants (fifth through eighth grade) is severely truncated. Second, the ability to detect project effectiveness is substantially reduced by so many youth transferring in and out of the target schools during the school year.

The positive results obtained to date suggest the value of further implementation and study of the LSP project. Future evaluation research on this project will assess the relationship between amount and type of service received in relationship to outcomes achieved. In addition, questions have been added to the survey to determine the length of time participants have been enrolled in each target school so that future cohort analyses control for amount of potential exposure to services. For example, average responses for participants with two or more years exposure to services should demonstrate superior outcomes compared to same grade participants with less than one year exposure.

# REFERENCES

Barrett, M. & Senay, E. (1990). Illinois Department of Alcoholism and Substance Abuse (IDASA) Youth Survey, 1990. Available from Addictions Research Institute, IDASA, Chicago, IL.

Bry, B.H. (1983). Empirical foundations of family-based approaches to adolescent substance abuse. In T.J. Glynn, C.G. Luekefeld, & J.P. Ludford (Eds.), Preventing adolescent drug abuse: Intervention strategies (pp. 154-171; NIDA Research Monograph No. 47). Washington, DC: U.S. Government Printing Office.

Cook, T.D. & Campbell, D.C. (1979). *Quasi-experimentation: design and analysis for field settings.* Rand McNally: Chicago.

Epstein, J.A., Botvin, G.J., Diaz, T. & Schinke, S.P. (1995). The role of social factors and individual characteristics in promoting alcohol use among inner-city minority youths, *Journal of Studies on Alcohol, 56,* 39-46.

Hawkins, J.D., Catalano, R.F., & Miller, J.Y. (1992). Risk and protective factors for alcohol and other drug problems in adolescence and early adulthood: implications for substance abuse prevention. *Psychological Bulletin, 112,* 64-105.

Johnston, L. (1994). Monitoring the Future Study, Available from the National Institute of Drug Abuse, Rockville, MD.

Maddahian, E., Newcomb, M.D., & Bentler, P.M. (1988). Adolescent drug use and intention to use drugs: concurrent and longitudinal analyses of four ethnic groups. *Addictive Behaviors, 13,* 191-195.

Murray, D.M., Richards, P.S., Luepker, R.V., & Johnson, C.A. (1987). The prevention of cigarette smoking in children: two and three year follow-up comparisons of four prevention strategies. *Journal of Behavioral Medicine, 10,* 595-611.

Olmedo, E.L. (1979). Acculturation: a psychometric perspective. *American Psychologist, 34,* 1061-1070.

Patterson, G.R, & Dishion, T.J. (1985). Contributions of families and peers to delinquency. *Criminology, 23,* 391-394.

Pentz, M.A., MacKinnon, D.P., Flay, B.R., Hansen, W.B., Wang, E.Y.I., & Johnson, C.A. (1989). A multi-community trial for primary prevention of adolescent drug abuse: effects on drug use prevalence. *Journal of the American Medical Association, 261,* 3259-3266.

Schinke, S.P., Botvin, G.J., & Orlandi, M.A. (1991). *Substance abuse in children and adolescents.* Newbury Park, CA: Sage Publications.

Van de Ven, A.H., & Ferry, D.L. (1980). *Measuring and Assessing Organizations.* New York: Wiley.

# Dosage-Related Changes in a Culturally-Responsive Prevention Program for Asian American Youth

Nolan Zane, PhD
Bart Aoki, PhD
Tamara Ho, BA
Lillian Huang, BA
Mike Jang, MA

**SUMMARY.** In an effort to provide more responsive modalities to treat and prevent alcohol and other drug (AOD) abuse in under-

Nolan Zane and Lillian Huang are affiliated with the Graduate School of Education, University of California, Santa Barbara, CA. Bart Aoki is affiliated with the Asian American Recovery Services, San Francisco, CA. Tamara Ho is affiliated with the Department of Psychology, California State University, Hayward. Mike Jang is affiliated with the Four Winds Research Corporation, San Francisco, CA.

Address correspondence to: Nolan Zane, Graduate School of Education, University of California, Santa Barbara, CA 93106-9490.

The authors thank Don Seeberg for the data analysis and Wendy Fong for assistance in the data collection. The contents of this article are the sole responsibility of the authors and do not necessarily represent the official views of the funding agency.

This evaluation study was supported by the Center for Substance Abuse, Grant 3-H86-SP04968 and by the National Research Center on Asian American Mental Health (National Institute on Mental Health Grant No. MH44331).

[Haworth co-indexing entry note]: "Dosage-Related Changes in a Culturally-Responsive Prevention Program for Asian American Youth." Zane, Nolan et al. Co-published simultaneously in *Drugs & Society* (The Haworth Press, Inc.) Vol. 12, No. 1/2, 1998, pp. 105-125; and: *Substance Abuse Prevention in Multicultural Communities* (ed: Jeanette Valentine, Judith A. De Jong, and Nancy J. Kennedy) The Haworth Press, Inc., 1998, pp. 105-125. Single or multiple copies of this article are available for a fee from The Haworth Document Delivery Service [1-800-342-9678, 9:00 a.m. - 5:00 p.m. (EST). E-mail address: getinfo@haworth.com].

served communities, intervention programs with an ethnic-specific focus have developed. However, there has been few empirical studies that examine the types of changes associated with participation in these programs. The present study examined the outcome changes associated with participation in the Competence Through Transitions (CTT) program, a prevention intervention specifically designed to serve the diverse needs of Asian American youth from five different Asian ethnic communities. The study identified aspects of the intervention that were related to outcome changes in order to better understand what accounts for the culturally responsive nature of this program. CTT participants were more knowledgeable about drugs and about the negative influences of drugs after completing the program during the school year. Also, there was a significant increase in school-based social comfort following participation in the program. For parents, there was a significant increase in school competence, but no significant change in their perception of family relations. CTT evinced much less effect on youth and family participants when the program was conducted in the summer in that no pre-post outcome changes were found for the summer-based intervention. The outcome differences between the two programs were found to be associated with specific types of *curriculum-based* dosage differences that were theoretically tied to those outcomes. The investigators discuss the ways in which the dosage differences between the school and summer programs may have contributed to the observed differences in outcomes. *[Article copies available for a fee from The Haworth Document Delivery Service: 1-800-342-9678. E-mail address: getinfo@haworth.com]*

## INTRODUCTION

The growing recognition of the need for culturally-responsive programs in the treatment and prevention of alcohol and other drug (AOD) abuse has led to a substantial increase of ethnically-specific interventions in ethnic minority communities (Bolek, Debro & Trimble, 1992; Catalano et al., 1993; Orlandi, 1992; Zane & Huh-Kim, 1994; Zane, Park, and Aoki, in press). As with other ethnic minorities, efforts to impact the Asian American communities have focused on creating programs with culturally-sensitive aspects that purportedly increase the effectiveness of the programs for this particular population (Kim, McLeod, & Shantzis, 1992; Zane & Huh-Kim, 1994). However, there has been a lack of empirical evidence on just how capable these programs are in effecting change in the particular communities for which they were designed; research has yet to show what specific aspects of these programs make them "culturally responsive" for Asian Americans. Studies are needed to not only test the effectiveness of these programs, but this research would also provide the empirical base for systematically developing more culturally competent interventions. Therefore, the evaluations of such programs must investigate both the changes that occur to participants as well as the features of the intervention that are associated with those changes (Catalano et al.; Yen, 1992).

A number of factors undoubtedly can contribute to the culturally-responsive nature of an intervention. One important feature may be the organizational structure from which these interventions are implemented in the target communities. Uba (1994) delineates three means by which Asian Americans receive mental health services: (1) through mainstream facilities by generally trained personnel, (2) through mainstream facilities by specially trained personnel, and (3) through segregated facilities by specially trained personnel. Research has given some indication that ethnic-specific services provided by bicultural, bilingual personnel in community-based agencies will tend to be utilized by Asian American clients (Sue, Zane, & Young, 1994). This configuration of services appears to be effective because it allows for institutional flexibility in program planning, utilizes efficiently those therapists who are culturally sensitive to Asian Americans, increases the visibility of services to the community, and apparently decreases the stigma associated with seeking help (Kim et al., 1992; Uba; Zane and Sasao, 1992).

Kim et al. (1992) describe six types of program activities that have been employed in community-based prevention programs for Asian Americans. Many of these models are based on AOD intervention theory and have been implemented without any outcome evidence of their effectiveness (Zane, Park & Aoki, in press). For example, a case management model addresses the basic needs of the client, using referrals to both formal service agencies and informal support networks to develop a system of care for the family. Such an approach might be particularly helpful to recent refugee and immigrant clients who may not know how to access formal organizations to help them with the problems they are facing. The goal of case management is to encourage a collaborative effort in developing a system of care for both the child and the family, while teaching self-advocacy and assessing natural support networks. Family-oriented interventions are based on the central importance of the Asian American family system to the psychosocial functioning of individuals (Sue & Morishima, 1982). Traditional East Asian cultures often emphasize prioritizing family needs over individual ones, and the context of strong, extended family support networks might help to prevent AOD abuse from occurring. However, research shows that family cohesion can both be a protective device as well as a social stressor for Asian Americans (Zane & Sasao). In a similar vein, the mutual support model is based on the collectivist nature valued in East Asian cultures. This support group strategy encourages the sharing of common experiences and the development of constructive alternatives in coping with daily stressors and acculturation pressures among the group members. Programs working from an information deficit model emphasize providing skills and information to treat the adjustment problems of Asian individuals. In this approach, the prevention agency and the provider become teachers and sources of information. These programs capitalize on the value placed in East Asian cultures on education by framing the interventions in an educational context. They work to clarify the meaning and consequences of drug taking behavior and to lessen the stigma associated with help-seeking. Empowerment models foster personal self-sufficiency by supporting a community's efforts to develop its own resources and the personal capabilities of its residents. Prevention programs that follow this model focus on the participant's abilities to seek solutions to their own problem, thereby, decreasing the personal alienation and helplessness that may lead to AOD use and abuse. Finally, a cultural enrichment approach focuses on reinforcing the bicultural or monocultural identification of individuals. It is based on the assumption that a lack of or weakening of cultural identification, whether with Asian or mainstream cultures, may create or exacerbate adjustment problems for Asian American individuals. This prevention strategy attempts to shape culturally valued characteristics to enhance cultural identification as a protective factor against AOD use and abuse.

Other types of interventions appear to have the potential to be useful as prevention programs for Asian Americans, but, again, these approaches have not been empirically validated (Zane & Sasao). For example, social skills programs would focus on increasing the ability of Asian American youth to interact more effectively with others. However, the development of what are considered Western-oriented social skills, such as open self-expression and assertiveness, might cause intra-familial tensions for Asian Americans because these individualistic-oriented behaviors may conflict with the emphasis placed on saving face and avoiding confrontations within such families. Although such programs may be effective for mainstream youth, further research is necessary to investigate their usefulness in Asian American communities. Peer model interventions are based on the premise that certain types of peer relationships might lead to or discourage AOD abuse, and these programs attempt to foster new or different peer relationships in which nonuse norms prevail among the peer group members. Evaluations of this type of intervention for Asians would determine if this approach is an effective means of intervention or whether other social contexts, such as the family, would be more culturally appropriate (Kim et al., 1992).

An important consideration in any prevention intervention for Asian Americans is the extent to which the intervention can accommodate or be adapted to address the specific needs of different Asian American ethnic groups. Past research has consistently documented heterogeneity with respect to substance use/abuse patterns and human service needs (Zane & Huh-Kim; Yen, 1992). Recognizing and addressing this heterogeneity may be vitally important because it appears that certain groups have higher risk factors (Southeast Asian refugees, Koreans, and Filipinos) for AOD abuse and that these particular groups constitute the most rapidly growing populations among Asian Americans (Zane & Sasao). Moreover, previous program evaluations have indicated that certain types of prevention strategies may be more effective in different Asian American communities (Asian Youth Substance Abuse Project, 1993). Thus evaluations of programs for Asian American communities must always account for this ethnic variation in the outcome studies. The present study examined the effectiveness of a prevention program specifically designed to serve the diverse needs of Asian American youth from five different Asian ethnic communities. The primary purpose of the study was to identify aspects of the intervention that were related to outcome changes in order to better account for the culturally responsive nature of this program.

## *METHOD*

### *Prevention Program and Participants*

Competence Through Transitions (CTT) is a substance abuse prevention program designed to increase the resiliency and protective factors of high risk Asian youth, ages 10 to 15, and their families as they approach and enter critical transitional periods. In order to address the ethnic diversity among the San Francisco Asian American communities, a network of seven community-based organizations are involved in the implementation of the CTT program. These agencies have a long history of collaboration, and have developed a strong, viable consortium which forms the stable basis for the CTT program. One agency served as the centralized administrative agent. It coordinates the prevention activities among the other agencies, conducts strategic planning and data gathering, and provides staff development training. Another agency has as its primary responsibility the provision of technical assistance to prevention staff in Asian American substance abuse issues and treatment and serves as the primary referral for treatment services when clients' problems have progressed to a point where a preventive approach is deemed inappropriate. The other five agencies are responsible for conducting the prevention interventions with five different Asian American communities: Chinese, Filipino, Japanese, Korean, and Vietnamese. Each agency conducts two prevention interventions, one during the school year and one during the summer.

The project's approach involves a combination of skill building and activity oriented interventions aimed at strengthening the ability of high risk Asian youths and families to more successfully accomplish specific school and cultural transitions. It attempts to involve Asian parents by appealing to their desire for their children to do well academically and by providing direct support for their increased effectiveness as parents in relation to school personnel and activities. Based at ethnic-specific youth centers, the project also emphasizes the importance of creating and strengthening cultural and community bonds for high risk youths. CTT emphasizes these areas because for Asian youths in the United States, developmental and cultural transitions are extremely critical. Asian youth and families are frequently ill-equipped to cope with the socio-developmental changes associated with these transitions as they occur in the context of American culture. Traditional Asian child-rearing practices emphasize academic performance rather than social involvement. Many Asian parents encounter difficulty with the need to balance flexibility with clear limit-setting to effectively parent the growing bicultural adolescent. With increasingly complex demands placed upon them, Asian youth often experience a sense of confusion and alienation from family members while at the same time lacking a network of supportive peers and mentors outside the home. During times of transition, crises arise that can lead to increasingly problematic and extreme behavior as the Asian youth and their family members are taxed beyond their limits.

Because parents and other family members will continue to play a significant role throughout the youth's life, the involvement and empowerment of all family members are particularly critical to the success of any prevention effort for Asians. Thus the project attempts to build on the importance of family and the strength inherent in the Asian parents' desire for the youth's success by directly involving and strengthening the parents' role in school settings. By supporting parental competence as well as embedding workshops and recreational activities in ethnic-specific youth and community centers in the neighborhoods, the competency of the youth are strengthened in a culturally affirming and enduring way.

CTT's overall goal is to increase the resiliency and protective factors of high risk Asian youth and their parents as the youth transition from elementary to middle school and from middle school to high school in order to reduce the likelihood that these youth will engage in alcohol, tobacco, and other drug (ATOD) use. At the individual level, the project's specific objectives are to (a) increase knowledge of critical youth health issues (drugs and HIV/AIDS), (b) enhance pro-social skills, and (c) increase cultural competence. At the family level, interventions are designed to enhance family relations among the youth and their parents. Finally, at the school level, CTT aims to generate more positive attitudes and social comfort for youth in school and to increase the parents' sense of efficacy in dealing with school-related issues and school personnel.

Prospective participants are designated as high-risk and eligible for participation in the program if they meet one or more of the following criteria: below C average; declining grades over two or more reporting periods; unexcused absence or lateness for three or more days per school year; parent-counselor conference for attendance or lateness problems; warning citation; individual detention; unsatisfactory citizenship grade; misconduct in class by teacher observation; parent-counselor conference for misconduct in class; suspension; pattern of regular tobacco use; signs of being under the influence of alcohol; initiation of other drugs; parental alcohol use (signs of being under the influence at least twice a month); parental use of other drugs.

The CTT approach consists of the following five intervention components, each tailored both developmentally and culturally to the specific needs of the acculturated and newcomer Asian youth participants: (a) Health Issues (gateway drugs and HIV/AIDS), (b) Transitional Social Competence, (c) Multicultural Competence, (d) Intergenerational Family Competence, and (e) School/Institutional Competence. Each component involves a series of workshops conducted by bilingual/bicultural health educators. The workshops are integrated into the activities of youth/community centers or are held in school settings. In order to give each participant individual attention, the groups are kept to a small, manageable number of 10 to 15 participants.

The Health Issues component is comprised of three 45-minute participatory sessions on gateway drugs and two 45-minute sessions on HIV/AIDS. The drug knowledge sessions address the myths and facts associated with gateway drugs, the process of addiction and related risk factors, and refusal skills. The HIV sessions focus on the myths and facts of HIV, the transmission process, high risk behaviors, protection against the virus, and how to relate to others with HIV or AIDS. The Transitional

Social Competence component is designed to enhance the social competence of youth in school settings, and it is comprised of four 45-minute skill building sessions. The topics include self-awareness and personal goals, problem solving, effective communication, and dealing with stress. The Multicultural Competence component is designed to generate greater cultural appreciation and pride among youth, and is comprised of three 45-minute participatory sessions focusing on cultural awareness, understanding and appreciating other cultures, and maximizing cultural strengths. The intergenerational Family Competence component aims to improve youth-parent relationships, and consists of interventions for youth and their parents. For the youth, four semi-structured meetings are organized around specific cultural events and family outings. Youth discussions primarily focus on familial values and intergenerational communication. Parent participants are involved in a series of small group (10 to 15 participants) workshops. Topics include familial values, limit setting and structure, encouragement, and intergenerational communication. Parent groups and multifamily activities are also supplemented on a selective basis with individual family meetings aimed at addressing needs specific to a particular family. The School/Institutional Competence component consists of four 1-hour parental meetings, a 45-minute youth session, and an on-site familial school orientation. The youth participate in a 45-minute session aimed at decreasing the youths' anxiety regarding attending a new school. The parent program focuses on improving a parent's effectiveness in dealing with school-related problems and institutional matters. Topics for the parent workshops include understanding the new school environment, parental rights and responsibilities, identifying and accessing community resources, and self advocacy and communication skills. In addition to these components, the youth participate in recreational activities and receive academic tutoring.

CTT conducted two prevention interventions, one during the 1994-95 school year and the other during the summer months of 1995. Pretest and posttest data were collected on 94 of the 105 registered youth in the school programs and on 51 of the 57 registered youth in the summer programs. Table 1 shows the demographic characteristics of the youth participants for the total CTT program and its member agencies. The program had mostly male participants, but two agencies, the Vietnamese and Japanese organizations, had substantial female participation. Consistent with CTT's emphasis, the program focused on intervening with preadolescent youth. With the exception of the Pan-Asian focus of the Japanese community agency, the CTT agencies tended to serve one particular Asian ethnic group. Finally, CTT served both newcomer and acculturated Asian youth, but there was great variation among the agencies in terms of this participant characteristic.

## Evaluation Design

As a part of the overall program evaluation of CTT, a pre-post design was implemented to examine the changes associated with participation in the youth and family interventions. Pre- and post-program assessments were made to determine if the interventions had achieved their specific objectives as indicated above. The intervention groups were pretested during the session prior to the implementation of the prevention activities and posttested after the final activity had been implemented. A process evaluation of how the curricula were implemented was also conducted to supplement the pre-post outcome study. Thirty percent of each agency's activities were randomly selected and observed by evaluation staff. The evaluators observed the extent to which curricula were implemented and documented any staff-related problems (e.g., lack of skill in group facilitation) or strengths (e.g., good rapport building skills) or external factors (e.g., pressure from agency administrators to change the program to better meet the service needs of that agency) that may have affected the implementation. Project staff were also interviewed about their perceptions of the participants and the activities.

## Measures

Table 2 lists the objective-related outcome measures, a brief description, and their psychometric properties. Previous evaluation studies of these measures have found them to be reliable with adequate concurrent validity (Zane, 1992; Zane & Chen, 1994). For example, as in the previous two years of the program, the measures were reliable with internal consistency alphas ranging from .65 to .93. The measures were translated and back translated. Discrepancies between the two forms were resolved by a three-person committee of bilingual experts. The youth and parent measures were available in English, Chinese, Korean, and Vietnamese, and were administered in the participant's primary language by the evaluation staff. Monolingual parents who were not literate were assisted by translators who had been trained in the assessment procedures.

## FINDINGS

### Program Dosage

Table 3 shows the average dosage (in minutes) of each major prevention activity that was received by youth in the school-year and summer

TABLE 1. CTT Cycle 3 Youth Demographics

| | Overall Program (N = 145) % (N) | CYC (N = 31) % (N) | JCYC (N = 21) % (N) | KCI (N = 24) % (N) | VYDC (N = 26) % (N) | WB (N = 43) % (N) |
|---|---|---|---|---|---|---|
| **Program** | | | | | | |
| School | 65% (94) | 81% (25) | 29% (06) | 62% (15) | 50% (13) | 81% (35) |
| Summer | 35% (51) | 19% (06) | 71% (15) | 38% (09) | 50% (13) | 19% (08) |
| **Sex** | | | | | | |
| Male | 61% (88) | 97% (30) | 29% (06) | 62% (15) | 38% (10) | 63% (27) |
| Female | 39% (57) | 3% (01) | 71% (15) | 38% (09) | 62% (16) | 37% (16) |
| **Age** | | | | | | |
| Preadolescent (10-12) | 67% (97) | 39% (12) | 71% (15) | 83% (20) | 46% (12) | 88% (38) |
| Midadolescent (13-15) | 33% (48) | 61% (19) | 29% (06) | 17% (04) | 54% (14) | 12% (05) |
| **Ethnicity** | | | | | | |
| Filipino | 30% (43) | | | | | 100% (43) |
| Chinese | 29% (42) | 94% (29) | 43% (09) | | 15% (04) | |
| Korean | 15% (22) | | | 92% (22) | | |
| Chinese-Vietnamese | 13% (19) | 6% (02) | 14% (03) | 4% (01) | 50% (13) | |
| Vietnamese | 7% (10) | | | 4% (01) | 35% (09) | |
| Asian-Mixed | 4% (06) | | 29% (06) | | | |
| Japanese | 1% (01) | | 5% (01) | | | |
| African-American | 1% (01) | | 5% (01) | | | |
| Other | 1% (01) | | 5% (01) | | | |
| **Acculturation Status** | | | | | | |
| Acculturated | 53% (77) | 0% (0) | 100% (21) | 96% (23) | 50% (13) | 46% (20) |
| Newcomer | 47% (68) | 100% (31) | | 4% (01) | 50% (13) | 54% (23) |
| **Place of Birth** | | | | | | |
| Born in U.S. | 34% (50) | 0% (0) | 95% (20) | 79% (19) | 19% (05) | 14% (06) |
| Born outside of U.S. | 66% (95) | 100% (31) | 5% (01) | 21% (05) | 81% (21) | 86% (37) |

CYC (Chinatown Youth Center); JCYC (Japanese Community Youth Council); KCI (Korean Center Incorporated); VYDC (Vietnamese Youth Development Center); WB (West Bay Pilipino Multi-Service Corporation)

114

TABLE 2. Characteristics of Intermediate Outcome Measures

| Domain | Instrument | Measure | Reliability M = avg. alpha R = range | Stand. for Population |
|---|---|---|---|---|
| **Health Issues** | Health Survey | Drug & HIV Knowledge | N/A | Yes |
| | Substance Use Inventory | Drug initiation? Use in past 30 days? | N/A | Yes |
| **Social Competence** | Personal Risk Behaviors Scale | School: Past 3 months? Summer: Past month? | M = .90 R = .87 to .93 | Yes |
| | Refusal Behaviors to Drugs & Peer Pressure Measure | How likely to be influenced by peers/family to use drugs and engage in negative behaviors? | M = .84 R = .83 to .86 | Yes |
| **Cultural Competence** | Cultural Appreciation Measure (Acculturated) | How much attachment and appreciation does youth have for his ethnic culture? | M = .84 R = .79 to .92 | Yes |
| | Cultural Pride Measure (Newcomers) | How much attachment and appreciation does youth have for his ethnic culture? | M = .75 R = .68 to .86 | Yes |

TABLE 2 (continued)

| Domain | Instrument | Measure | Reliability M = avg. alpha R = range | Stand. for Population |
|---|---|---|---|---|
| **Family Competence** | Youth-Parent Relations Measure (Youth) | How supportive is family? Frequency of pos. and neg. parental interactions. | M = .85 R = .87 to .93 | Yes |
| | Youth-Parent Relations Measure (Parents) | How supportive is family? Frequency of pos. and neg. youth interactions. | M = .77 R = .65 to .88 | Yes |
| **School Competence** | School-based Social Comfort Scale | How often does youth feel anxious in social & school situations? | M = .88 R = .82 to .92 | Yes |
| | School Competence Measure (Parents) | How effective does parent feel in school situations? | M = .78 R = .72 to .83 | Yes |

TABLE 3. Total and Curriculum-Based Dosage Comparisons Between the School and Summer Programs

| Activity | Total Dosage | | | Curriculum-based Dosage | | |
|---|---|---|---|---|---|---|
| | Mean | Std. Dev. | t | Mean | Std. Dev. | t |
| **Drugs & HIV** | | | | | | |
| School | 188.51 | 111.32 | −6.59*** | 182.60 | 107.46 | −6.01*** |
| Summer | 353.52 | 190.58 | | 335.30 | 198.76 | |
| **Social Competence** | | | | | | |
| School | 352.12 | 204.06 | −3.53** | 304.30 | 160.53 | 0.42 |
| Summer | 512.16 | 341.52 | | 292.45 | 164.46 | |
| **Cultural Competence** | | | | | | |
| School | 257.23 | 130.71 | .93 | 127.66 | 68.18 | −2.04 |
| Summer | 235.88 | 134.60 | | 154.41 | 87.11 | |
| **Family Competence** | | | | | | |
| School | 60.10 | 102.04 | 1.51 | 41.80 | 69.90 | 4.05*** |
| Summer | 35.59 | 75.30 | | 1.77 | 12.60 | |
| **School Competence** | | | | | | |
| School | 163.93 | 66.79 | 1.61 | 147.81 | 55.81 | 6.79*** |
| Summer | 145.49 | 64.20 | | 90.59 | 30.29 | |
| **Recreation** | | | | | | |
| School | 1283.46 | 1311.63 | −8.50*** | — | — | — |
| Summer | 4407.47 | 617.17 | | — | — | |
| **Tutoring** | | | | | | |
| School | 545.27 | 1170.13 | −.64 | — | — | — |
| Summer | 669.70 | 1033.41 | | — | — | |

Note: School N = 94. Summer N = 51.
**p < .01, ***p < .001 (2-tail tests).
Numbers refer to minutes of programming.

programs in Year 3. It is evident that certain activities were given more emphasis in the programs. For school-year programs, social and cultural competence interventions were provided at greater dosages compared with drug knowledge training and school competence interventions. Family competence was provided at the lowest level of dosage. As expected, the non-curriculum activities, recreation and tutoring had the highest level of dosage. A similar pattern of dosage was found for the summer programs with social and cultural competence having the higher levels of dosage. Drug knowledge training was also provided at a high dosage level, but much of this increase resulted from implementation of a supplemental HIV/AIDS education program in the summer months. As indicated in Table 3, school year and summer programs differed in dosage with respect to a number of prevention activities. Compared with the summer program, the school-year program had lower dosages in drug knowledge training, social competence, and recreation. Most of the difference in drug knowledge programming can be attributed to a funding artifact. Additional HIV/AIDS workshops were introduced by CTT in the summer due to the project's receipt of a supplemental HIV/AIDS grant. The other differences in activity dosage most likely reflect actual program variations in programming. It should be noted that the dosage levels reported here refer to the total time provided to each youth that was considered by staff to address a certain intervention area. Both curriculum and non-curriculum based intervention are included in these totals. When only curriculum-based programming is considered, differences between programs are even more marked. These differences will be presented and discussed in a subsequent section of the results.

### Pre-Post Intervention Changes

The four ethnic-specific and one Pan-Asian programs of CTT completed their Year 3 cycles in September 1995. Each program conducted two prevention interventions, one during the 1994-1995 school year and the other during the summer months of 1995. Pretest and posttest data were collected on 94 of the 105 registered youth in the school programs and on 51 of 57 registered youth in the summer programs. The attrition rates (10.4% for school and 10.5% for summer) were not substantial, and comparable to the attrition found in Year 2 (9.4%). Analyses were conducted on the intermediate objective-related outcome measures to examine changes for the CTT youth following the school-year and summer programs.

*School programs.* Table 4 shows the pre-post mean comparisons of the various intermediate outcome measures for the school programs. A significant change was found in the youth's knowledge about drugs. Participants were more knowledgeable about drugs and about the negative influences of drugs after completing the CTT program. Also, there was a significant increase in school-based social comfort following participation in the program. No significant changes were found for cultural pride, cultural appreciation, personal risk behaviors, and relationships with one's parents. There was a significant decrease in refusal behaviors (to drugs). With respect to personal risk behaviors and drug use, significant pre-post

TABLE 4. Pre- and Posttest Comparisons on Intermediate Outcomes for School Program

|  | Pretest | | Posttest | | | |
|---|---|---|---|---|---|---|
| Domain | M | SD | M | SD | df | t |
| **Health Issues** | | | | | | |
| Drug & HIV Knowledge | 16.79 | 3.00 | 18.48 | 3.27 | 93 | −5.16*** |
| Substance Use Inventory[A] | | | | | | |
| Initiation of Cigarettes | 1.83 | .378 | 1.74 | .438 | 93 | 2.61* |
| Initiation of Alcohol | 1.73 | .444 | 1.67 | .473 | 93 | 1.51 |
| Initiation of Other Drugs | 0.23 | .725 | 0.13 | .477 | 93 | 1.41 |
| Cigarette Use (past mo.) | 1.32 | 1.03 | 1.29 | .863 | 93 | .46 |
| Alcohol Use (past mo.) | 1.19 | .422 | 1.18 | .463 | 93 | .23 |
| Other Drug Use (past mo.) | 1.07 | .253 | 1.01 | .082 | 93 | 2.09* |
| **Social Competence** | | | | | | |
| Personal Risk Behaviors[B] | 61.14 | 6.91 | 60.99 | 7.44 | 93 | .26 |
| Refusal Behaviors to | | | | | | |
| Drugs & Peer Pressure | 34.47 | 5.35 | 33.39 | 5.58 | 93 | 2.49* |
| **Cultural Competence** | | | | | | |
| Cultural Appreciation | | | | | | |
| (Acculturated youth) | 27.76 | 3.97 | 26.22 | 4.43 | 40 | 1.70 |
| Cultural Pride | | | | | | |
| (Newcomer Youth) | 23.00 | 3.66 | 22.64 | 3.36 | 52 | .68 |
| **Family Competence** | | | | | | |
| Youth-Parent Relations (Youth) | 56.66 | 10.19 | 55.61 | 10.79 | 93 | 1.56 |
| Youth-Parent Relations (Parents) | 59.50 | 6.43 | 59.82 | 4.09 | 27 | −.33 |
| **School Competence** | | | | | | |
| School-based Social Comfort | | | | | | |
| (Youth) | 50.29 | 11.56 | 54.49 | 10.69 | 93 | −4.03*** |
| School Competence (Parents) | 27.03 | 6.98 | 30.60 | 6.90 | 27 | −3.15** |

Note: *$p$ < .05, **$p$ < .01, ***$p$ < .001 (2-tail tests).
Higher numbers refer to a greater level of that variable, except as noted below:

[A] Substance use initiation: 1 = used; 2 = never used.
Substance use during past month: 1 = no use; a higher number indicates more frequent use.
[B] Personal Risk Behaviors Scale: A lower number indicates higher risk.

change was found for the initiation of cigarette smoking and for the frequency of other drug use (not cigarette or alcohol use) in the past month; there was a greater initiation of smoking but less other drug use following participation in the program. For parents, there was a significant increase in school competence, but no significant change in their perception of family relations.

The pattern of changes found in the intermediate outcome data is somewhat consistent with the programming emphases observed in the CTT school-year programs. As shown in Table 3, the greatest dosage of *curric-*

*ulum-based* interventions received by participants involved interventions focused on social or school competence ($M = 452.11$ minutes) followed by drug knowledge training ($M = 182.60$ minutes) whereas relatively less programming was done in the areas of cultural competence and family issues ($M = 127.66$ and $41.80$ minutes, respectively). This difference in dosage may partially explain why positive effects were found for drug knowledge/awareness and for school-based social comfort but not for youth-parent relations or cultural appreciation and cultural pride. With respect to the cultural competence measures, ceiling effects may have occurred because youth reported high levels of pride and appreciation of their ethnic cultural background at pretest. Considered from this context, the program appeared to maintain cultural pride during a developmental period in which many youth tend to reject or question their cultural heritage. The increase in initiating cigarette smoking may be due to more youth experimenting during this developmental period, as this experimenting effect has been found for drug prevention programs that increase youths' knowledge and awareness of drugs. It is also possible that the decrease in refusal behaviors may reflect this greater tendency to experiment with cigarettes. The decrease in the frequency of other drug use was most likely the result of usage reduction in only a very small number of youth because the mean use levels were already quite low at pretest.

   *Summer programs.* Pre-post changes on the intermediate outcomes measures for the summer CTT programs are displayed in Table 5. Only one significant outcome change was observed, namely that youth participants reported less use of drugs other than alcohol or nicotine at the posttest. Again, as in the school-year programs, the very low usage levels at pretest indicate that this change in substance use most likely resulted from a reduction by only a very small number of youth. The lack of changes in the summer program raises the possibility that the summer participants may have been at less risk than the school participants, in which case the former group's level of functioning on many of the competence-based measures may have been already too high (or too low on the risk-based measures) for the program to appreciably affect. Comparisons of the two intervention groups on pretest functioning do not support this hypothesis as few differences were found between the groups. The differences that were found suggest that the summer youth participants were at slightly higher risk. Compared with the school-year participants, summer youth were less knowledgeable about drugs (summer $M = .70$ correct, $SD = .12$; school $M = .78$ correct, $SD = .13$), $t(143) = 3.59$, p $< .001$, and reported poorer family relations (summer $M = 53.29$, $SD = 8.78$; school $M = 56.66$, $SD = 10.18$), $t(143) = -1.99$, $p < .05$. Also, the summer group was rated by the preven-

TABLE 5. Pre- and Posttest Comparisons on Intermediate Outcomes for Summer Program

| Domain | Pretest | | Posttest | | | |
|---|---|---|---|---|---|---|
| | M | SD | M | SD | df | t |
| **Health Issues** | | | | | | |
| Drug Knowledge | 11.67 | 1.89 | 11.20 | 2.57 | 50 | 1.64 |
| Substance Use Inventory[A] | | | | | | |
| Initiation of Cigarettes | 1.88 | .328 | 1.86 | .351 | 49 | .57 |
| Initiation of Alcohol | 1.66 | .479 | 1.66 | .479 | 49 | .00 |
| Initiation of Other Drugs | 2.50 | 1.51 | 1.88 | 1.12 | 7 | 1.49 |
| Cigarette Use (past mo.) | 1.16 | .784 | 1.18 | .793 | 50 | −1.00 |
| Alcohol Use (past mo.) | 1.17 | .385 | 1.22 | .461 | 50 | −.70 |
| Other Drug Use (past mo.) | 1.08 | .214 | 1.02 | .065 | 49 | 2.19* |
| **Social Competence** | | | | | | |
| Personal Risk Behaviors[B] | 60.41 | 7.77 | 60.78 | 7.78 | 50 | −.45 |
| Refusal Behaviors to | | | | | | |
| Drugs & Peer Pressure | 33.50 | 5.29 | 33.18 | 5.30 | 50 | 66 |
| **Cultural Competence** | | | | | | |
| Cultural Appreciation | | | | | | |
| (Acculturated youth) | 25.56 | 4.18 | 25.20 | 5.27 | 33 | .52 |
| Cultural Pride | | | | | | |
| (Newcomer Youth) | 23.71 | 3.50 | 22.79 | 5.80 | 13 | .69 |
| **Family Competence** | | | | | | |
| Youth-Parent Relations (Youth) | 53.29 | 8.78 | 53.41 | 8.77 | 50 | −.12 |
| Youth-Parent Relations (Parents) | 57.67 | 5.44 | 60.73 | 6.00 | 14 | −2.03 |
| **School Competence** | | | | | | |
| School-based Social Comfort | | | | | | |
| (Youth) | 51.72 | 9.50 | 51.37 | 11.86 | 50 | .35 |
| School Competence (Parents) | 27.93 | 7.98 | 29.47 | 7.06 | 14 | −.88 |

Note:  *p < .05 (2-tail tests).
Higher numbers refer to a greater level of that variable, except as noted below:

[A] Substance use initiation: 1 = used; 2 = never used.
Substance use during past month: 1 = no use; a higher number indicates more frequent use.
[B] Personal Risk Behaviors Scale: A lower number indicates higher risk.

tion staff as having more high risk characteristics at intake (summer $M$ = 2.63, $SD$ = 1.76; school $M$ = 1.81, $SD$ = 1.35), $t(143)$ = 3.14, p < .01.

*Process Findings*

Qualitative observations indicated that there was a great deal of variance across the five agencies regarding curricula implementation. These observations were generally corroborated by staff interviews that were conducted at the end of the school program by evaluation staff. Two agencies attempted to strictly adhere to the outlined curriculum, covering all of the key points and implementing the stated activities and role plays. Observations, however, revealed that in some of the sessions youth management problems prevented staff from implementing the full curriculum module. Two other agencies seemed to focus on relaying the general themes of the individual curriculum modules to their participants. These two agencies generally implemented about half of the listed activities. This strategy allowed the groups to go more in depth in one or two chosen interventions as opposed to briefly touching on a number of activities. The remaining agency tended to use the curriculum as a listing of possible discussion topics that could be used in a general discussion format. This strategy appeared to foster group retainment and bonding, but may have been less effective at reaching the intermediate outcome areas targeted for change.

## DISCUSSION

CTT participants were more knowledgeable about drugs and about the negative influences of drugs after completing the CTT program. Also, there was a significant increase in school-based social comfort following participation in the program. No significant changes were found for cultural pride, cultural appreciation, personal risk behaviors, and relationships with one's parents. There was a significant decrease in refusal behaviors (to drugs). With respect to personal risk behaviors and drug use, significant pre-post change was found for the initiation of cigarette smoking and for the frequency of other drug use (not cigarette or alcohol use) in the past month; there was a greater initiation of smoking but less other drug use following participation in the program. For parents, there was a significant increase in school competence, but no significant change in their perception of family relations. CTT evinced much less effect on youth participants when programs were conducted in the summer. A number of explanations can be considered on how dosage differences could have mitigated the effect of the summer program. First, the summer program actually placed less emphasis on curriculum programming in relation to non-curriculum activities, particularly recreation. The summer program had more than 3.5 times the amount of recreational activity compared with the school-year program. From this perspective, summer youth received relatively lower dosages of prevention activities designed to specifically change behaviors and attitudes. Second, the greater emphasis on recreation may reflect the fact that in the summer, many youth are not oriented to the school-oriented curricula of CTT and, consequently, may be less responsive to the prevention interventions. Third, it is also possible that with school not being in session, the summer participants did not have an adequate opportunity to use and practice the social skills and refusal behaviors in critical situations that are more often found in the school settings. These possibilities strongly suggest that the school-based curricula of the CTT program may have required more modification to accommodate situational and youth attitudinal changes that often occur during the summer months. CTT was originally conceived and designed to impact school adjustment which would then serve as a protective factor against drug involvement. Most of its curricula were designed to focus on school-related issues. Dosage data suggests that the summer programs were more recreation-oriented and this combined with the possibly "non-school" attitudes of the youth and the lack of the school milieu to serve as a relevant learning environment may have mitigated the effect of CTT during the summer. The CTT experience strongly suggests that school based curricula must be significantly modified to better fit the social conditions of the summer months when such interventions are implemented outside of the school year.

The positive effects of CTT's school program relative to its summer interventions are only suggestive in view of the lack of a control group in the outcome study. It is possible that maturation and history influences instead of the program may have accounted for these changes especially given the differences in program duration and time of administration between the school and summer programs. However, the outcome differences between the two programs were found to be associated with specific types of *curriculum-based dosage* differences that were theoretically tied to those outcomes (e.g., family dosage differences were related to program differences in parent sense of school competence). It appears that school program effects are a more parsimonious explanation of this pattern than either maturation or history effects.

In examining the relationship between dosage and outcomes, it appears that the distinction between curriculum based training and non-curriculum interventions is a useful one. In CTT, more interpretable differences between the summer and school programs were observed when curriculum based exposure rather than total minutes spent on a particular intervention was used. Qualitative observations indicate that there was variance in how the prevention interventions were implemented. This variance would become even more problematic for effective implementation when the curricula were not used. The school based program showed more effects on intermediate outcomes and this may be partially due to the fact that the school based program had relatively more curriculum based programming relative to non-curriculum based programming.

Finally, it appears that in consortium based projects, such as CTT, the variability among agencies in implementation becomes a critical program challenge. Qualitative observations indicated that there was a great deal of variance across the five agencies regarding curricula implementation. Individual agencies should vary the implementation to fit the specific needs of the targeted youth groups, and this is especially true for Asian American communities in which there exists great heterogeneity among the ethnic specific populations. On the other hand, significant variation in the implementation of the intervention activities can result in muted impact because the programs may not be having similar effects due to the variance in how they implement the interventions. It would be informative for future evaluation efforts to systematically examine how implementation variance is related to intermediate and ultimate outcomes. In this manner, evaluations of purportedly culturally-responsive programs such as CTT can be more definitive about which aspects of the program actually are associated with the desired outcome changes.

## REFERENCES

Asian Youth Substance Abuse Project. (1993). *Final Report.* Washington, D.C.: Office for Substance Abuse Prevention.

Bolek, C.S., Debro, J., & Trimble, J.E. (1992). Overview of selected efforts to encourage minority drug abuse research and researchers. In J.E. Trimble, C.S. Bolek, & S.J Niemcryk (Eds.), *Ethnic and Multicultural Drug Abuse: Perspectives on Current Research.* New York: Harrington Park Press, pp. 345-375.

Catalano, R.F., Hawkins, J.D., Krenz, C., Gillmore, M., Morrison, D., Wells, E., & Abbot, R. (1993). A guide to culturally appropriate drug abuse prevention. *Journal of Consulting and Clinical Psychology, 61,* 804-811.

Kim, S., McLeod, J.H., & Shantzis, C. (1992). Cultural competence for evaluators working with Asian-American Communities: Some practical considerations. In *Cultural competence for evaluators: A guide for alcohol and other drug abuse prevention practitioners working with ethnic/racial communities* Rockville, MD: U.S. Department of Health and Human Services (DHHS), pp. 203-260.

Orlandi, M.A. (1992). The challenge of evaluating community based-prevention programs: A cross-cultural perspective. In *Cultural competence for evaluators: A guide for alcohol and other drug abuse prevention practitioners working with ethnic/racial communities* Rockville, MD: U.S. DHHS, pp. 1-22.

Sue, S. & Morishima, J.K. (1982). The Mental Health of Asian Americans. San Francisco: Jossey-Bass.

Sue, S., Zane, N., & Young, K. (1994). Research on psychotherapy with culturally diverse populations. In A. Bergin & S. Garfield (Eds.), *Handbook of psychotherapy and behavior change* (4th ed.). New York: John Wiley & Sons.

Uba, L. (1993). *Asian Americans: Personality patterns, identity, and mental health.* New York: Guilford Publications.

Yen, S. (1992). Cultural competence for evaluators working with Asian/Pacific American communities: Some common themes and important implications. In *Cultural competence for evaluators: A guide for alcohol and other drug abuse prevention practitioners working with ethnic/racial communities* Rockville, MD: U.S. DHHS, pp. 261-291.

Zane, N., & Chen, E. (1994). *Year-end report for Youth Scope.* United Cambodian Community: Unpublished report.

Zane, N. (1992). *Renewal report for the evaluation of Competence Through Transitions.* Asian American Recovery Services: Unpublished report.

Zane, N. & Huh-Kim, J. (1994). Substance use and abuse among Asian Pacific Americans. In N. Zane, D. Takeuchi, & K. Young (Eds.), *Confronting critical health issues of Asian and Pacific Islander Americans.* Newbury Park, CA: Sage Publications.

Zane, N., Park, S., & Aoki, B. (in press). The development of culturally-valid measures for assessing prevention impact in Asian communities. In M.A. Orlandi, R. Weston, & L.G. Epstein (Eds.), *Cultural competence for evaluators.* (Vol 2). Rockville, MD: Center for Substance Abuse Prevention.

Zane, N. & Sasao, T. (1992). Research on drug abuse among Asian Pacific Americans. In J.E. Trimble, C.S. Bolek, & S.J. Niemcryk (Eds.), *Ethnic and Multicultural Drug Abuse: Perspectives on Current Research.* New York: Harrington Park Press, p. 181-209.

# Strengthening Causal Inference in Adolescent Drug Prevention Studies: Methods and Findings from a Controlled Study of the Urban Youth Connection Program

Jeanette Valentine, PhD
John Griffith, PhD
Robin Ruthazer, MS
Barbara Gottlieb, MD
Stefano Keel, MSW

**SUMMARY.** *Introduction.* The Urban Youth Connection represents a model substance abuse prevention program implemented in an

Jeanette Valentine was affiliated with the Department of Pediatrics, Division of General Pediatrics and Adolescent Medicine and The New England Health and Poverty Action Center, New England Medical Center, Boston, MA. John Griffith and Robin Ruthazer are affiliated with the Department of Internal Medicine, Division of Clinical Care Research, Biostatistics Research Center, New England Medical Center, Boston, MA. Barbara Gottlieb and Stefano Keel are affiliated with the Brookside Community Health Center, Brigham and Women's Hospital, Boston, MA.

Address correspondence to: Jeanette Valentine, PhD, Children's Hospital Medical Center, 4800 Sand Point Way, Box CM-09, Seattle, WA 98101.

Support for this study was provided by the Center for Substance Abuse Prevention, Substance Abuse and Mental Health Administration, Health Services Resource Administration, U.S. Public Health Service: CSAP Grant No. 5H 86-SP02902. The contents of this article are the sole responsibility of the authors and do not necessarily represent the official views of the funding agency.

[Haworth co-indexing entry note]: "Strengthening Causal Inference in Adolescent Drug Prevention Studies: Methods and Findings from a Controlled Study of the Urban Youth Connection Program." Valentine, Jeanette et al. Co-published simultaneously in *Drugs & Society* (The Haworth Press, Inc.) Vol. 12, No. 1/2, 1998, pp. 127-145; and: *Substance Abuse Prevention in Multicultural Communities* (ed: Jeanette Valentine, Judith A. De Jong, and Nancy J. Kennedy) The Haworth Press, Inc., 1998, pp. 127-145. Single or multiple copies of this article are available for a fee from The Haworth Document Delivery Service [1-800-342-9678, 9:00 a.m. - 5:00 p.m. (EST). E-mail address: getinfo@haworth.com].

urban public middle school and high school serving predominantly Hispanic and African American students. The program provided counseling, mentoring and academic support. Findings from the evaluation are presented in this paper.

*Methods.* A pre-test, post-test comparison group design estimated the impact of the program on ultimate outcomes of 30-day use of alcohol, tobacco and other drugs, and intermediate outcomes of risk behaviors, psychosocial well-being, and school involvement, as measured by self-administered questionnaires given each fall and spring from 1993-1996. A non-equivalent comparison group was drawn from non-participants at each school. The data analysis strategy relied on a multivariate model comparing ultimate and intermediate outcomes at follow-up among treatment and comparison students after adjustment for demographic, baseline risk differences, and program exposures differences for treatment students.

*Results.* The follow-up rate for treatment students at the middle school was 71% (n = 78), and 48% at the high school (n = 109). The comparison group students (n = 135 at the middle school and n = 308 at the high school) differed from the treatment group on selected demographic and behavioral measures at baseline. Unadjusted outcomes at follow-up were significantly worse in the treatment group than in the comparison group. Statistical adjustment eliminated significant differences between the treatment and comparison groups at follow-up, and higher program exposure was associated with better outcomes for some measures.

*Discussion.* Adjustment for differences between treatment and comparison groups and correction for variation in program exposure within the treatment group are essential for accurate estimation of the benefits of drug prevention interventions. *[Article copies available for a fee from The Haworth Document Delivery Service: 1-800-342-9678. E-mail address: getinfo@haworth.com]*

## INTRODUCTION

The use of illegal drugs in the teen years has been rising since the early 1990s (Johnston, O'Malley, and Bachman, 1995). The most recent report of The Monitoring the Future Study of Johnston et al., which provides annual estimates of daily, yearly, and lifetime use of alcohol, tobacco and drugs among America's eighth, tenth and twelfth grade students, indicates rising rates of marijuana and other drug use since 1991, but notes that the prevalence in the 1990s remains far below the peak rates observed in the 1970s. The proportion of eighth-graders reporting any illicit drug use in the preceding 12 months rose from 11% in 1991 to 21% in 1995. Among tenth-graders, 33% reported illicit drug use in 1995, compared to 20% in

1992. Illicit drug use among high school seniors increased from 27% in 1992 to 39% in 1995. Use of tobacco has continued to show a modest increase since the early 1990s. The use of alcohol in the adolescent student population in America is not showing an increase in the 1990s, but remains unacceptably high, at prevalence estimates of 15%, 24%, and 30% for eighth, tenth, and twelfth grade students respectively in 1995.

The use of alcohol, tobacco and other drugs (ATOD) by youth often co-occurs with a wide range of adolescent risk behaviors which constitute the major threats to adolescent health, such as early and unprotected sexual intercourse, weapon-carrying, physical fighting, and gang involvement (Gans et al., 1990, and U.S. Office of Technology Assessment, 1991). The Centers for Disease Control and Prevention (1995) estimate that 72% of all deaths among adolescents are from four leading causes which have significant behavioral and psychosocial components: motor vehicle crashes, unintentional injuries, homicide, and suicide. The 1993 Youth Risk Behavior Surveillance Systems reported a lifetime use of alcohol among high school students of 80.9%, a 32.8% lifetime use of marijuana, and 30.5% of high school students considered current smokers (Centers for Disease Control and Prevention, 1995). These behavioral health problems of America's adolescents must be addressed by multidisciplinary health interventions. The evidence is increasing that adolescent risk behaviors are co-occurring, with important gender differences that should be accounted for in service programs (Dukarm et al., 1996, and Wilson and Joffe, 1995). Aggressive and violent behavior is associated with substance use and other adolescent risk behaviors (Orpinas, Engquist, Grunbaum, and Parcel, 1995), and these relationships differ for males and females (Valois, McKeown, Garrison, and Vincent, 1995).

Empirical and theoretical formulations of predictors of substance use and abuse among adolescents suggest that an individual's social, psychological and behavioral characteristics can pose a risk of substance abuse (Levitt, Selman, and Richmond, 1991). Interventions aimed at promoting resiliency factors, such as effective coping skills, stress management, and positive self-esteem and identity, can contribute to reduced incidence and prevalence of substance abuse and related unhealthy behaviors.

The need to identify cost-effective interventions to prevent and reduce substance abuse among youth is great. Policymakers and service providers look to evaluation research to provide answers to critical questions of what works and for whom. The challenges to maximizing scientific rigor in field-based settings are great. Demand for services can preclude random assignment. Risk status of participants often means lower school or program attendance, thus creating high lost-to-follow-up rates. Wide variations in underlying risk profiles of participants can lead to wide variations in program benefits, thus canceling out any measurable program impact for participants as a whole. These problems can have important consequences for analysis and interpretation. Incomplete data, small sample size, and insufficient technical resources for complex, multivariate data analysis, can impose limitations on the ability of a prevention program to identify program benefits.

This paper presents the methods and findings from an outcome evaluation of a model substance abuse prevention program that provided counseling services to students attending a public middle school and high school in Boston, Massachusetts. The aim of the study was to estimate the effectiveness of a model adolescent drug prevention program in a scientifically rigorous manner, employing a quasi-experimental study design in lieu of an experimental study design that proved impossible for ethical and political reasons. The methods and findings from the outcome evaluation provide a model approach to estimating the impact of field-based demonstration projects on adolescent substance abuse prevention and reduction.

## THE INTERVENTION

### Services

The core services of the Urban Youth Connection Program consist of individual, pair or group counseling provided to students attending a middle school and a high school in Boston during the period 1993-1995 for the middle school, and 1993-1996 at the high school. At the middle school site, students in grade 7 initiated service and were encouraged to continue to participate until graduation in grade 8. At the high school site, the services of the intervention were offered to students in all grades. Services in both sites were offered only during the academic year beginning in October each year and ending in May. Students from both sites were from predominantly Hispanic and African American backgrounds. Students entered the program initially through referral from teachers, based upon a risk profile of academic risk, behavioral problems in the classroom, and other identified mental health or behavioral concerns. After the initial program year, new and continuing students participated based upon self-referrals as well as teacher referral. Counseling services are provided by graduate student interns enrolled in a masters degree program in educational psychology at a local university. In addition to compensation, the counseling interns receive academic credit for their full year of service in this program. The counselors are supervised by two full-time clinical supervisors with other administrative responsibilities for the intervention. Four counselors at the middle school and five counselors at the high school are available 15 hours per week, of which seven hours are dedicated clinical time. The remaining hours include training, supervision, administrative work, parent/teacher contact, and client outreach. Upon referral to the program, students are offered an opportunity to participate. After parental permission is obtained, students are placed in individual, pair or group counseling based upon an intake assessment.

During the two-year service period at the middle school (October 1993-May 1995), a total of 110 students participated in the services of the Urban Youth Connection, out of a total population of 275 seventh and eighth graders at the school during this time. At the high school site, a total of 227 students from all four grades participated in the services of the Urban Youth Connection during the three-year service period (October 1993-May 1996), out of a population of 1200 students on average during this time period.

### Service Dosage

Program intakes began as early as October and continued as late as March in each of the two years. Thus, length of time in the program and, relatedly, the number of visits possible, varied widely among participants. At the middle school, program participants received an average of 16.7 visits during the two year study period (range of 1-47, SD = 11.7). Length of time in the program, defined as the amount of time between the date of the first recorded service activity and the date of the last recorded activity, averaged 7.8 months, with a range of .03 months to 19.6 months (SD = 6.1). Core counseling visits, defined as an individual, paired, or group counseling visit, averaged 8.3 individual counseling visits per student, 8.8 paired counseling visits per student, and 10.9 group counseling visits per individual student. The remainder of service contacts–non-counseling visits–included intake interviews, parent/teacher meetings, and advocacy meetings or telephone calls. Thus, the majority of service contact was for counseling purposes.

At the high school site, program participants received over 3000 service visits over the three year study period and averaged 16.4 visits per participants overall (range of 1-72, SD = 12.6). High school participants received an average of 6.4 individual counseling visits. Of those who participated in paired counseling at the high school site, participants averaged 9.5 paired counseling visits during this time period. High school participants averaged 11.3 group counseling visits during the three year study period.

Length of time in the program at the high school averaged 9.9 months per participants, with a range of .03 months to 31.7 months (SD = 8.0).

## OUTCOME STUDY METHODS

### Study Design

A pre-test, post-test comparison group design was used to estimate the influence of the model program on adolescent substance use and related outcomes. The treatment group was composed of all students who attended the program for at least one visit for an assessment and intake. The comparison group students were drawn from students who attended the same school but did not receive any services. In the case of the seventh grade students, the entire seventh grade class was given a self-adminis-tered questionnaire in the classroom setting in the fall of the 1993 school year (early November) and again in the spring of the 1994 school year (late April). The seventh grade cohort was followed into grade eight, and two school-based surveys were conducted in the fall and spring of the 1994-1995 school year. Since program enrollment continued throughout the school year, students were classified at the end of the school years as either treatment or comparison group students, depending on whether or not they participated in the program during the two-year study period. At the high school, two classrooms at each grade level were randomly se-lected as the comparison group, and surveys were administered in class-room settings in the fall and spring each year of the three-year study period commencing September 1993 through June 1996. The treatment group students completed the questionnaire shortly after intake for the baseline and in May and June for the follow-up, either individually or in small groups. Subject retention was accomplished by conducting two surveys per year over the course of the two and three year study periods at each site, with the intent of obtaining at least one baseline and one follow-up survey per student to maximize the sample size over time. Within-school comparison groups were constructed to assure that the treatment and com-parison groups would be as demographically comparable as possible. Comparability of populations across schools is especially difficult in Bos-ton because of out-of-district student placements due to court-mandated busing. A multivariable model was constructed to address possible selec-tion bias caused by non-equivalent comparison groups at each site.

The major outcomes of interest are self-reported 30-day use of alcohol, tobacco, and other drugs (ultimate outcomes) and other outcomes associated with substance use: self-esteem, social coping, depression, interpersonal violence, school involvement, school attendance, and academic performance (intermediate outcomes). Program inputs included number of service visits and duration of time in treatment. Two levels of service intensity were constructed as the major independent variable. A student was classified as having "high exposure to the intervention" if his or her total number of visits exceeded the median number of visits for the overall treatment group *and* the length of time in the program exceeded the median number of months in service for the treatment group as a whole. All other treatment students who did not fall above the median on both of these measures were classified as having "low exposure to the intervention." Students' participation in the survey was voluntary, and parents had the right to exclude their children from the survey. The study protocol was approved by the institutional review board of the service organization.

### Study Sample

For the purposes of the outcome study, a treatment student is defined as a student for whom a Client Intake was completed and documented, who received at least one service from the Urban Youth Connection Program during the study period, and for whom a baseline and follow-up survey are available ("paired survey group"). Program participants for whom follow-up data are available represent a subset of the total treatment population. The paired survey treatment group at each site was compared to the non-paired treatment group students on demographic characteristics of age, gender, racial background, and living arrangement, service dosage (length of time in the program and number of visits), and initial risk profile, with "high risk" defined as previous history of substance use/abuse, court involvement, and history of mental health treatment, and "low risk" defined as no history of these factors.

Results of statistical tests comparing paired survey treatment group students with non-paired survey treatment group students are presented in Table 1. A total of 78 paired treatment group surveys were available for analysis at the middle school site, which represents 71% of the 110 middle school students who participated in the program during the 1993-1995 school years. At the high school site, a total of 109 paired treatment group surveys were available for analysis, representing 48% of the total treatment population of 226 during the study period 1993-1996. At the middle school site, the paired survey treatment group is significantly different from the non-paired treatment group on only one demographic measure: racial distribution, with African American over-represented and Hispanic under-represented in the paired survey group. There are no differences in risk status at intake between paired and non-paired survey treatment group students at the middle school. At the high school site, the paired survey sample is comparable to the non-paired survey group on all four demographic measures, as well as risk profile at intake. Paired survey-takers are more likely than non-paired survey-takers to have received more UYC service visits and participated longer (p < .001 for both measures at both program sites, Table 1). Thus, at both sites, the treatment students for whom a follow-up survey is available are representative of treatment students for whom a follow-up survey was not available in terms of demographic and risk variables. The final study sample, however, tended to receive more services than those who did not complete follow-up surveys.

A comparison group student is defined as a student who did not participate in the Urban Youth Connection Program during the study period and for whom both baseline and follow-up surveys are available. At the middle school site, 135 students were classified as comparison group students. At the high school site, 308 paired surveys were available in the comparison group. Table 2 compares demographic characteristics of treatment and comparison group paired survey-takers at each site.

At the middle school site, the treatment group differs from the comparison group in the overall racial distribution, with the treatment group having a higher proportion of African American students, and the comparison group having a higher proportion of Hispanic students (p < .001). Living situation is statistically significantly different for the treatment group than for the comparison group: there is a higher proportion of students from single parent homes among the treatment group than in the comparison group (p < .05). A marginally significant difference was found between treatment and comparison group in mean age, with the comparison group slightly younger than the treatment group (p < .10).

At the high school site, the treatment and comparison paired survey groups do not differ on any demographic measure except gender distribution. The treatment group has more male students than the comparison group (62% vs. 43%, p < .01). Statistically significant demographic differences between treatment and comparison paired survey-takers at both sites will be adjusted for in the multivariable model.

## Measurement

Exposure to the intervention is a measure that combines the number of visits with the length of time in the program, both of which were calculated from all visits recorded on service log forms. Participants were classified as having high exposure to the intervention if their number of visits and length of time in the program exceeded the median number of visits and median length of time in the program. All other participants

TABLE 1. Comparison of Paired Survey-Takers* and Non-Paired Survey-Takers on Demographic Characteristics, Service Dosage, and Risk Status at Intake, by Program Site. Urban Youth Connection: Program Participants 1993-1996

| Variable | Middle School | | | High School | | |
|---|---|---|---|---|---|---|
| | Paired (n = 78) | Non-paired (n = 32) | p-val. # | Paired (n = 109) | Non-paired (n = 117) | p-val. # |
| **Demographics** | | | | | | |
| Age: mean (std. dev.) | 12.7 (2.2) | 13.2 (2.6) | .38 | 15.4 (2.9) | 15.1 (3.8) | .53 |
| Gender n(%) | | | .68 | | | .78 |
| female | 38 (49%) | 17 (53%) | | 41 (38%) | 171 (57%) | |
| male | 40 (51%) | 15 (47%) | | 66 (62%) | 131 (43%) | |
| Race | | | .043 | | | .54 |
| African-American | 32 (42%) | 6 (19%) | | 29 (27%) | 24 (21%) | |
| Asian | 3 (4%) | 0 (0%) | | 4 (4%) | 3 (3%) | |
| Hispanic | 28 (37%) | 21 (66%) | | 57 (54%) | 62 (53%) | |
| White | 6 (8%) | 1 (3%) | | 3 (3%) | 8 (7%) | |
| Other | 7 (9%) | 4 (13%) | | 13 (12%) | 20 (17%) | |
| Living Situation | | | .27 | | | .37 |
| neither Parent | 3 (4%) | 4 (13%) | | 8 (8%) | 4 (4%) | |
| single Parent | 40 (56%) | 17 (55%) | | 53 (54%) | 54 (52%) | |
| both Parents | 28 (39%) | 10 (32%) | | 37 (38%) | 45 (44%) | |
| **Service Dosage** | | | | | | |
| Median # Days (Interquartile Range) | 188 (96-220) | 84 (1-153) | .001 | 194 (129-384) | 124 (34-205) | .001 |
| Median # Visits (Interquartile Range) | 15 (7-23) | 4.5 (1-12) | | 15 (9-22) | 8 (3-15) | |
| **Risk Status at Intake**\*\* | | | .87 | | | .52 |
| high Risk | 37 (49%) | 15 (47%) | | 56 (55%) | 55 (50%) | |
| low risk | 39 (51%) | 17 (53%) | | 46 (45%) | 54 (50%) | |

* Paired survey = students for whom both a baseline and follow-up survey are available and who utilized program services between baseline and follow-up survey completion

** High Risk = students who had history of previous mental health treatment, court involvement, or substance use, at intake
   Low Risk = students who had no history of previous mental health treatment, court involvement, or substance use, at intake

# p-values from t-test (age) or Chi-square test (all other demographic and risk characteristics), Wilcoxon RaNk-sum Test (service dosage)

TABLE 2. Comparability of Paired-Survey Treatment and Comparison Group Students on Demographic Characteristics at Baseline, by Program Site. Urban Youth Connection: 1993-1996

| Variable | Middle School | | | | High School | | | |
|---|---|---|---|---|---|---|---|---|
| | Trt (n = 78) | | Comp (n = 135) | p-val. # | Trt (n = 109) | | Comp (n = 308) | p-val. # |
| Age mean (std.dev.) | 12.9 (.8) | | 12.6 (.9) | .0506 | 16.0 (1.5) | | 16.2 (1.5) | .29 |
| Gender n (%) | | | | .86 | | | | .001 |
| female | 38 | (49%) | 66 (50%) | | 41 | (38%) | 171 (57%) | |
| male | 40 | (51%) | 66 (50%) | | 66 | (62%) | 131 (43%) | |
| Racial Distribution | | | | .001 | | | | .103 |
| African American | 32 | (42%) | 19 (15%) | | 29 | (27%) | 101 (34%) | |
| Asian | 3 | (4%) | 2 (2%) | | 4 | (4%) | 12 (4%) | |
| Hispanic | 28 | (37%) | 81 (63%) | | 57 | (54%) | 117 (39%) | |
| White | 6 | (8%) | 13 (10%) | | 3 | (3%) | 20 (7%) | |
| Other | 7 | (9%) | 14 (11%) | | 13 | (12%) | 48 (16%) | |
| Living Situation | | | | .019 | | | | .54 |
| Neither Parent | 5 | (7%) | 15 (11%) | | 14 | (13%) | 29 (10%) | |
| Single Parent | 45 | (59%) | 52 (39%) | | 52 | (49%) | 141 (48%) | |
| Both Parents | 26 | (34%) | 66 (50%) | | 40 | (38%) | 125 (42%) | |
| Maternal Education | | | | .36 | | | | .39 |
| < high school | 20 | (27%) | 32 (24%) | | 37 | (36%) | 83 (28%) | |
| high school grad | 13 | (17%) | 26 (20%) | | 22 | (21%) | 83 (28%) | |
| some college/trade | 20 | (27%) | 23 (17%) | | 25 | (24%) | 75 (25%) | |
| don't know | 22 | (29%) | 51 (39%) | | 19 | (18%) | 60 (20%) | |
| Paternal Education | | | | .34 | | | | .16 |
| < high school | 16 | (22%) | 22 (17%) | | 22 | (22%) | 71 (25%) | |
| high school grad | 12 | (16%) | 12 (9%) | | 13 | (13%) | 56 (19%) | |
| some college/trade | 9 | (12%) | 22 (17%) | | 19 | (19%) | 68 (23%) | |
| don't know | 37 | (50%) | 71 (56%) | | 44 | (45%) | 95 (33%) | |

# p-values from t-test (mean age) or Chi-square test (all other demographic variables)

were classified as having low exposure. The program exposure variables were recorded on the following program record forms: intake form, individual service log, and group service log. These tools were designed for purposes of the evaluation and were completed daily by the counseling staff. Quality assurance reviews were conducted to assure completeness, accuracy, and consistency of recordings, and all records were entered into a computerized database that was then linked to the self-administered student questionnaires.

A broad range of behavioral and attitudinal outcomes were measured by a 139-items self-administered questionnaire given to treatment and comparison school students two times per year over the course of the service years at each site. The impact of exposure to the intervention was assessed on ultimate outcomes and three categories of intermediate outcomes. Ultimate outcomes included self-reported 30-day use of alcohol, tobacco and other drugs. The first group of intermediate outcomes measured were the following risk behaviors: 30-day weapon-carrying, 30-day physical fighting, gang membership, arrest history. A second group of intermediate outcomes included psychosocial measures of suicidal ideation, clinical depression, self-esteem score, and social coping score. A third group of intermediate outcome measures included indicators of school involvement and school bonding. The self-administered questionnaire incorporated questions from the Center for Disease Control's Youth Risk Behavior Survey, as well as scales whose reliability and validity have been established to assess self-esteem, social coping and depression. Self-esteem was measured using the Hare Self-esteem Scale (Hare 1985). Social coping was assessed through the Shorkey Whiteman Rationality Inventory (Whiteman and Shorkey, 1978), which can be used to assess level of functioning as well as change. Depression was assessed using the 30-item Children's Depression Inventory (CDI) of Maria Kovacs (Kovacs, 1985), which provides an index of severity and can measure change. The two data sets–service records and self-reported surveys–were linked together by means of a unique alphanumeric identifier to carry out the outcome analyses.

### Data Analysis Strategy

Testing differences in self-reported behavioral and psychosocial outcomes among treatment and comparison group students at follow-up, after adjusting for demographic differences and initial baseline status on the key outcome measures, was the primary strategy for data analysis. Since the comparison groups at both sites are not equivalent to the treatment group, the multivariate analysis adjusted for differences in the demographic profile between treatment and comparison group. The method of survey administration, which involved periodic surveys in the classrooms during the service period, created differences in the interval, or length of time elapsed, between the first survey and the follow-up survey, and there were statistically significant differences in the interval between baseline and follow-up between treatment and comparison group students at both sites, but in different directions at each site. The treatment group in the middle school was more likely than the comparison group to have had a shorter interval elapse between baseline and follow-up. At the high school level, the reverse is true. The treatment group students at the high school are more likely than the comparison group to have had a longer interval between baseline and follow-up. Since the amount of time elapsing between baseline and follow-up is significantly different for treatment and comparison group students, this variable is controlled for in the final multivariable model.

Table 3 presents results of statistical tests comparing the treatment group and comparison group students at baseline on 30-day ATOD, risk behaviors, psychosocial well-being measures, and school involvement measures. At the $p < .05$ level, the treatment group at the middle school site is significantly higher than the comparison group at baseline on five measures: 30-day use of beer, 30-day weapon-carrying, suicidal ideation, usual grades of c, d, f, and school suspension. At the high school, the treatment group is significantly worse than the comparison group at baseline on eight outcome measures: 30-day hard liquor use, 30-day beer use, 30-day weapon-carrying, previous arrest, lower self-esteem, usual grades in school C or lower, lower proportion hope to finish college, and higher proportion suspended from school. Thus, the treatment and comparison groups at both program sites are not comparable to each other in terms of risk at baseline. Initial differences at baseline on the ultimate and intermediate outcomes of interest are controlled for in the multivariate logistic regression model which is used here to compare the treatment and comparison groups at the follow-up period, which occurs after a variable length of exposure to the intervention.

A multivariable model was constructed using logistic regression to adjust for statistically significant differences between the treatment group and the non-equivalent comparison group. Ultimate and intermediate outcomes among treatment group students at follow-up were compared to the same outcomes among non-exposed comparison group students, after controlling for demographic differences between the two groups, initial status at baseline on ultimate and intermediate outcomes, and length of the interval between the first and last surveys. The adjusted odds ratios were calculated from a multivariable logistic regression model which included age, race, living situation, time between first and last survey, and the baseline status of the outcome variable as covariates. Amount of exposure to the intervention was stratified into any exposure, low exposure, and high exposure.

TABLE 3. Comparability of Paired-Survey Treatment and Comparison Groups on Ultimate and Intermediate Outcomes at Baseline, by Program Site. Urban Youth Connection: 1993-1996

| Variable | Middle School | | | High School | | |
|---|---|---|---|---|---|---|
| | Trt (n = 78) | Comp (n = 135) | p-val. # | Trt (n = 109) | Comp (n = 308) | p-val. # |
| Ultimate Outcomes | % | % | | % | % | |
| *30-day ATOD: (% yes)* | | | | | | |
| hard liquor | 5.4 | 4.6 | .81 | 33.6 | 19.3 | .003 |
| beer | 40.8 | 19.7 | .001 | 51.9 | 38.9 | .020 |
| wine | 31.2 | 27.5 | .58 | 34.6 | 29.1 | .30 |
| wine cooler | 31.2 | 20.8 | .093 | 35.2 | 31.0 | .43 |
| tobacco | 25.3 | 15.2 | .072 | 30.8 | 25.7 | .31 |
| marijuana | 12.2 | 8.5 | .40 | 25.5 | 20.5 | .29 |
| inhalant | 7.9 | 5.3 | .47 | 0.9 | 2.0 | .47 |
| cocaine | 2.7 | 1.5 | .57 | 1.0 | 1.0 | .97 |
| Intermediate Outcomes | | | | | | |
| *Risk Behaviors:* | | | | | | |
| carried weapon | 30.3 | 17.6 | .034 | 36.3 | 18.6 | .001 |
| physical fight | 38.5 | 26.7 | .073 | 20.2 | 13.0 | .073 |
| gang member | 7.7 | 3.7 | .22 | 9.6 | 5.7 | .17 |
| been arrested | 32.5 | 32.6 | .99 | 31.4 | 19.9 | .016 |
| *Psychosocial Status:* | | | | | | |
| think about killing self | 33.3 | 18.1 | .033 | 36.4 | 27.1 | .101 |
| clin. depress ( > 60 cdi) | 15.5 | 15.0 | .94 | 17.4 | 15.0 | .60 |
| self-esteem (mean) | 86.7 | 89.3 | .078 | 85.5 | 88.6 | .007 |
| social coping (mean) | 17.6 | 17.8 | .86 | 19.9 | 19.3 | .35 |
| *School Involvement:* | | | | | | |
| Usual grades c,d,f | 39.4 | 19.4 | .002 | 56.3 | 36.3 | .001 |
| think about drop out | 5.2 | 1.5 | .13 | 10.2 | 5.0 | .057 |
| hope to finish college | 77.0 | 84.1 | .21 | 70.8 | 81.4 | .022 |
| cut class very often | 2.7 | 0.8 | .28 | 7.4 | 4.0 | .16 |
| suspended from school | 42.9 | 21.1 | .001 | 55.6 | 35.1 | .001 |

# p-values from t-test (self-esteem and social coping scores) or Chi-square test (all other ultimate and intermediate outcome variables)

# RESULTS

## Crude, Unadjusted Outcomes Among Treatment and Comparison Group at Follow-Up

The crude, unadjusted outcomes among treatment and comparison group students at the follow-up, presented in Table 4, indicate that the treatment group is significantly higher than the comparison group on selected outcomes at both sites. The intervention program has served students who are high risk, with the non-equivalent comparison group representing a broader range of risk than the treatment group. For the middle school, there were no statistically significant differences between treatment and comparison group students at follow-up on any measures of 30-day ATOD. On the risk behaviors, the treatment group was significantly more likely than the comparison group to report weapon-carrying (p = .037), and being a member of a gang (p = .047) than were comparison group students. No statistically significant differences were found on measures of psychosocial well-being between treatment and comparison group students. On measures of school involvement, the treatment group was more likely to report usual grades of c, d, and f, than were comparison group students (p = .012). Treatment group students were significantly more likely to report a school suspension than were comparison group students (p = .001). At the high school site, the treatment group students were significantly more likely to report 30-day hard liquor use than were comparison group students (38.9% vs. 21.5%, p = .001), as well as marijuana use (38.5% vs. 20.2%, p = .001). Marginally significant differences were found between treatment and comparison group students at the high school on beer and wine use, with the treatment group reporting higher rates of use than the comparison group (p = .007 for both). The treatment group was significantly more likely to report all four risk behavior measures than were the comparison group students: weapon-carrying, physical fighting, gang membership, and previous arrest. Treatment group students had a statistically significantly lower mean self-esteem score than did the comparison group (85.9 vs. 88.6, p = .032). Treatment group students were significantly more likely to report lower overall grades, less likely to hope to finish college, frequent class-cutting, and school suspension, than were the comparison group students. Marginally significant differences in the percent of students considering dropping out of school were found between treatment and comparison, with the treatment students having a higher proportion reporting "thinking about dropping out."

## Adjusted Outcomes Among Treatment and Comparison Group Students at Follow-Up

Table 5 presents the results of the multivariable model which compares outcomes at follow-up between treatment and comparison group after

TABLE 4. Crude, Unadjusted Prevalence Rates of Ultimate and Intermediate Outcomes Among Paired-Survey Treatment and Comparison Group Students at Follow-Up, by Program Site. Urban Youth Connection: Paired Survey Takers, 1993-1996

| | Middle School | | | High School | | |
|---|---|---|---|---|---|---|
| Variable | Trt (n = 78) | Comp (n = 135) | p-val. # | Trt (n = 109) | Comp (n = 308) | p-val. # |
| Ultimate Outcomes | % | % | | % | % | |
| *30-day ATOD: (% yes)* | | | | | | |
| hard liquor | 9.6 | 11.3 | .71 | 38.9 | 21.5 | .001 |
| beer | 40.5 | 32.6 | .26 | 53.2 | 38.3 | .007 |
| wine | 28.4 | 32.1 | .58 | 38.9 | 25.3 | .007 |
| wine cooler | 33.8 | 27.8 | .37 | 30.6 | 32.3 | .74 |
| tobacco | 21.9 | 21.6 | .97 | 30.3 | 22.6 | .12 |
| marijuana | 18.1 | 9.9 | .10 | 38.5 | 20.2 | .001 |
| inhalant | 6.8 | 2.2 | .11 | 1.8 | 1.7 | .92 |
| cocaine | 0.0 | 1.6 | .29 | 1.9 | 0.7 | .29 |
| Intermediate Outcomes | | | | | | |
| *Risk Behaviors:* | | | | | | |
| carried weapon | 30.0 | 17.3 | .037 | 32.1 | 18.9 | .005 |
| physical fight | 28.8 | 26.9 | .77 | 24.3 | 14.3 | .018 |
| gang member | 16.4 | 7.5 | .047 | 13.2 | 6.4 | .027 |
| been arrested | 33.3 | 35.1 | .81 | 41.1 | 21.8 | .001 |
| *Psychosocial Well-being:* | | | | | | |
| think about killing self | 25.0 | 22.4 | .71 | 30.8 | 22.8 | .13 |
| clin. depress ( > 60 cdi) | 15.6 | 15.3 | .96 | 17.5 | 15.7 | .68 |
| self-esteem (mean) | 87.0 | 89.7 | .11 | 85.9 | 88.6 | .032 |
| social coping (mean) | 17.8 | 19.4 | .13 | 20.5 | 19.9 | .35 |
| *School Involvement:* | | | | | | |
| Usual grades c, d, f | 34.7 | 18.9 | .012 | 67.6 | 42.1 | .001 |
| think about drop out | 5.3 | 5.2 | .98 | 11.9 | 6.3 | .063 |
| hope to finish college | 70.3 | 79.9 | .12 | 68.2 | 82.9 | .001 |
| cut class very often | 4.1 | 5.3 | .69 | 19.6 | 5.7 | .001 |
| suspended from school | 49.3 | 24.6 | .001 | 62.4 | 39.5 | .001 |

# unadjusted p-values from t-test (self-esteem and social coping scores) or Chi-square test (all other ultimate and intermediate outcome variables)

adjusting for statistically significant differences between the treatment and comparison groups on demographic characteristics, length of interval between the pre-test and post-test survey, and status at baseline of the outcome variable. Shown in Table 5 are the adjusted odds ratios resulting from the multivariable logistic regression models for each outcome, with the comparison group classified as having 0 program participation, and the treatment group classified as any program participation, low program participation, and high program participation. An odds ratio of greater than one indicates the odds of the outcome are higher in the treatment group than the comparison group. An odds ratio of less than one indicates the odds of the outcome are lower in the treatment group than the comparison group. For the middle school, the results of statistical adjustment eliminate any statistically significantly higher rates of 30-day ATOD in the treatment group at low, high, and any program exposure level. The adjusted odds ratio for 30-day use of beer indicates that the treatment group which had a high level of program participation reported statistically significantly lower rates of 30-day beer use than the comparison group (Adj. O.R. = 0.2, 95% p < .05). After statistical adjustment, the treatment group with low exposure at the middle school is still significantly more likely than the comparison group to report weapon-carrying and school suspension. The treatment group with any exposure is higher in gang membership, and is more likely to report school suspension. Overall, the results of the multivariable model which adjusts for the significant differences in the non-equivalent comparison group at the middle school suggest that the intervention has led to improvements in outcomes from the baseline period, since differences between treatment and comparison groups are eliminated at follow-up after statistical adjustment. The significant differences that remain after adjustment are apparent for behavioral indicators associated with interpersonal violence—weapons, gang involvement, and school suspension. For the subgroup of students who received high exposure to the intervention, however, there are no statistically significant differences in the violence-related indicators between treatment and comparison group, thus suggesting that participants can benefit if they have more exposure to the intervention. The positive benefit of high program participation on lower beer use is also promising.

At the high school level, where the crude, unadjusted outcomes indicated much higher negative outcomes among the treatment group, statistical adjustment has reduced the number of negative outcomes that are statistically significantly higher for the treatment group, and has shown some positive benefits in terms of academic aspirations. However, treatment group students with any level of program participation were signifi-

TABLE 5. Adjusted Odds Ratios [+] for Ultimate and Intermediate Outcomes Among Paired-Survey Treatment vs. Comparison Group Students at Middle School and High School Sites, Stratified by Level of Program Exposure. Urban Youth Connection: Paired Survey-Takers, 1993-1996

| | Middle School | | | High School | | |
|---|---|---|---|---|---|---|
| Variable | Level of Program Exposure[++] | | | Level of Program Exposure[++] | | |
| | Any vs. 0 | Low vs. 0 | High vs. 0 | Any vs. 0 | Low vs. 0 | High vs. 0 |
| | Adj. O.R. | Adj. O.R. | Adj. O.R. | Adj. O.R. | Adj. O.R. | Adj. O.R. |
| **Ultimate Outcomes** | | | | | | |
| *30-day ATOD* | | | | | | |
| hard liquor | 1.0 | 0.9 | 1.3 | 1.6 | 1.6 | 1.7 |
| beer | 0.8 | 1.5 | 0.2** | 1.3 | 1.2 | 1.6 |
| wine | 0.6 | 0.8 | 0.4 | 2.7** | 3.0** | 2.2 |
| wine cooler | 0.8 | 0.7 | 1.0 | 0.8 | 1.0 | 0.5 |
| tobacco | 0.6 | 0.6 | 0.6 | 1.7 | 1.8 | 1.6 |
| marijuana | 2.2 | 2.2 | 2.2 | 3.7** | 2.4* | 6.2** |
| **Intermediate Outcomes** | | | | | | |
| *Risk Behaviors* | | | | | | |
| Weapon-carry (30-day) | 2.4 | 3.2* | 1.5 | 1.3 | 1.7 | 0.9 |
| Physical Fight (30-day) | 0.9 | 0.6 | 1.6 | 1.4 | 1.4 | 1.5 |
| Gang Membership | 2.8* | 3.0 | 2.5 | 1.9 | 1.8 | 2.0 |
| *Psychosocial Well-being* | | | | | | |
| Suicidal Ideation | 0.5 | 0.7 | 0.3 | 1.2 | 2.3 | 0.4 |
| Clinical Depression | 0.9 | 0.5 | 1.5 | 1.0 | 0.9 | 1.1 |
| | Parameter Estimate[+++] | | | Parameter Estimate[+++] | | |
| Self-esteem Mean Score | + 1.7 | + 3.0 | + 0.8 | − 0.3 | + 0.6 | − 1.6 |
| Coping Mean Score | + 0.4 | − 0.1 | + 1.0 | + 0.4 | + 0.7 | + 0.2 |
| | Adj. O.R. | Adj. O.R. | Adj. O.R. | Adj. O.R. | Adj. O.R. | Adj. O.R. |
| *School Involvement* | | | | | | |
| Usual grades c, d, e | 1.4 | 1.9 | 0.9 | 2.6** | 2.1* | 3.3** |
| Consider dropping out | 0.7 | 0.6 | 0.9 | 1.3 | 1.6 | 0.9 |
| Hope to finish college | 0.5 | 0.4 | 0.8 | 0.4** | 0.5* | 0.3** |
| Suspended from school | 3.0** | 5.1** | 1.0 | 1.5 | 1.1 | 2.2 |

[+]Adjusted results are from a multivariable logistic regression model which included age, race, living situation, time between first and last survey, and the baseline status of the outcome variable as covariates. An odds ratio (OR) > 1 indicates the odds of the outcome are higher in the treatment group than in the comparison group. An OR < 1 indicates the odds of the outcome are lower in the treatment group than in the comparison group.

[++]High program exposure = students with # of days of service and number of visits exceeding the median for both measures. Low exposure = all other treatment group students. Any exposure = all treatment group students. Zero program exposure = comparison group students.

[+++]Parameter estimate > 0 indicates the control score is higher. Parameter estimate < 0 indicates the treatment score is higher.

** p-value < 0.05, statistically significant difference between treatment and comparison groups
* p-value < 0.10, marginally significant difference between treatment and comparison groups

cantly more likely than the comparison group to report 30-day use of wine (Adj. O.R. = 2.7, p < .05), with the low participation group significantly different from the comparison group, but not for participants with a high level of program participation. Self-reported 30-day use of marijuana was significantly higher for all program participants, whether high or low exposure, than among comparison group students. While there were significant differences in interpersonal violence measures before statistical adjustment between treatment and comparison groups, after statistical adjustment the treatment and comparison groups do not differ on these measures. Program participants are more likely to report overall lower grades than are comparison group students, even after statistical adjustment. However, program participants, especially those with high exposure, are more likely to report aspirations to complete college than are comparison group students (Adj. O.R. for high program participation vs. comparison group = 0.3, p < .05).

## DISCUSSION

The outcome study of the Urban Youth Connection suggests some important benefits of program participation inferred from shifts in statistical significance after adjustment. The intervention aids in reducing 30-day use of beer at the middle school level, and hard liquor, beer, and wine use in the high school group. Treatment students show an improvement in risk behaviors related to interpersonal violence and academic involvement. High program exposure is a key factor in impacting outcomes for high risk youth. The guiding philosophy of the Urban Youth Connection program is harm reduction, thus acknowledging the high risk status of participants at intake. Harm reduction is defined as prevention of the downward spiral of negative consequences of substance use and other high risk behaviors, and promotion of self-esteem and positive peer networks. There are also opportunities for primary prevention among those participants who have not yet initiated harmful health behaviors. Qualitative information from teacher and staff interviews identified the strong collaborative relationship of the program with the schools, the acceptance of each participant at his or her unique stage of health, the gender-specific counseling, and staff role modeling as key elements of success.

The study design implications are that adolescent drug prevention studies should include hypotheses consistent with reduction in negative outcomes between baseline and follow-up, not just primary prevention of onset. Data analysis techniques should take into account variations within both the treatment and comparison groups. Key to more accurate estimation of program impact is the establishment of an integrated program utilization and outcome database that can be drawn on to adjust for case mix severity and to take into account differences in service utilization levels. Outcomes should include behavioral, psychosocial and functional measures.

## REFERENCES

Centers for Disease Control and Prevention (1995). Youth Risk Behavior Surveillance-United States, 1993. MMWR March 24.

Dukarm, C.P., Byrd, R.S., Auinger, P., & Weitzman, M. (1996). Illicit Substance Use, Gender, and the Risk of Violent Behavior Among Adolescents. Arch. of Pediatric and Adolescent Medicine 150, 797-801.

Gans, J.G., & Blythe, Dale A., Elster, A.B., & Gaveras, L.L. (1990). America's adolescents: How healthy are they? Chicago, Ill.: American Medical Association.

Hare BR (1985). Hare Self-Esteem Scale. Unpublished Manuscript, Department of Sociology, SUNY Stony Brook, New York (mimeo). Available from The Free Press.

Johnston LD, O'Malley PM, and Bachman JG (1995). National Survey Results on Drug Use from the Monitoring the Future Study, 1975-1995. Rockville, MD: National Institute on Drug Abuse.

Kovacs, Maria (1985). The Children's Depression Inventory. Pharmacology Bulletin 21(4): 995-998.

Levitt MZ, Selman RL, and Richmond JB (1991). The Psychosocial Foundations of Early Adolescents' High Risk Behavior: Implications for Research and Practice. J of Research on Adolescence 1(4): 349-378.

Sosin DM, Koepsell TD, Rivara FP (1995). Fighting as a Marker for Multiple Problem Behaviors in Adolescents. J of Adolescent Health 16: 209-215.

U.S. Office of Technology Assessment (1991). Adolescent Health. Volume I: Summary and Policy Option. Washington, D.C.: U.S. Government Printing Office.

Valois RF, McKeown RE, Garrison CZ, and Vincent ML (1995). Correlates of Aggressive and Violent Behaviors Among Public High School Adolescents. J of Adolescent Health 1: 26-34.

Whiteman VL, and Shorkey CT (1978). Validation Testing of the Rational Behavior Inventory. Educational and Psychological Measurement 38: 1143-1149.

Wilson MD, and Joffe A (1995). Adolescent Medicine. J of American Medical Association 21: 1657-1659.

# Prevention Through Empowerment in a Native American Community

Eva L. Petoskey, MS
Kit R. Van Stelle, MA
Judith A. De Jong, PhD

**SUMMARY.** This article describes a work in progress. It reports on a prevention demonstration grant program which combined several complementary strategies: a school-based cultural curriculum, training of teachers, development of a leadership core group, and a community curriculum, in an effort to address the self-perception of personal and communal powerlessness of Native Americans, which places them at risk for drug and alcohol abuse. A student survey was used to examine substance use, school bonding and the relationship between cultural affiliation and substance use for the youth population. Two sets of outcome results, quantitative and qualitative, are reported and discussed in relation to the Freirian model of community

Eva L. Petoskey is affiliated with the First American Prevention Center, Bayfield, WI. Kit R. Van Stelle is affiliated with the University of Wisconsin, Center for Health Policy & Program Evaluation. Judith A. De Jong is currently an independent consultant acting as a grant writer and evaluator on adolescent prevention programs, Lanham, MD.

Address correspondence to: Eva L. Petoskey, 2848 Setterbo Road, Suttons Bay, MI 49682.

The authors would like to thank Bonnie M. Duran, DrPH for helpful discussions on empowerment.

This study was supported by the Center for Substance Abuse Prevention (Grant #1H86SPO2205). The contents of this article are the sole responsibility of the authors and do not necessarily represent the official views of the funding agency.

[Haworth co-indexing entry note]: "Prevention Through Empowerment in a Native American Community." Petoskey, Eva L., Kit R. Van Stelle, and Judith A. De Jong. Co-published simultaneously in *Drugs & Society* (The Haworth Press, Inc.) Vol. 12, No. 1/2, 1998, pp. 147-162; and: *Substance Abuse Prevention in Multicultural Communities* (ed: Jeanette Valentine, Judith A. De Jong, and Nancy J. Kennedy) The Haworth Press, Inc., 1998, pp. 147-162. Single or multiple copies of this article are available for a fee from The Haworth Document Delivery Service [1-800-342-9678, 9:00 a.m. - 5:00 p.m. (EST). E-mail address: getinfo@haworth.com].

*147*

empowerment. *[Article copies available for a fee from The Haworth Document Delivery Service: 1-800-342-9678. E-mail address: getinfo@haworth.com]*

## INTRODUCTION

The concept of empowerment and its opposite, powerlessness, has been used in a variety of contexts. On the psychological level, concepts such as: external locus of control, learned helplessness, alienation, lack of a sense of coherence within one's environment, and internalized oppression have been used to describe individual powerlessness (Wallerstein, 1992). In community psychology literature, Wallerstein notes elements on the collective level: "communities achieving equity of resources; having both equity and the capacity to solve problems; identifying their own problems and solutions; increasing participation in community activities leading to improved neighborhoods, a stronger sense of community, and personal and political efficacy, and developing a participatory social action model to increase the effectiveness of natural helping systems and supporting proactive behaviors for social change" (1992).

Paulo Freire (1970) related the individual and communal concepts, identifying the following elements as critical to empowerment: improved self concept, critical analysis of the world, identification with members of a community, participating in, organizing for and carrying out environmental change.

In its simplest terms, personal empowerment must be more than individual improvement of skills or increase in self-esteem. If the individual is truly unable to exert control over the circumstances in his or her environment, attempts to change the psychological outlook of the individual can actually intensify the awareness of and feeling of powerlessness over life circumstances (Wallerstein, 1992, p. 198).

In an application funded by CSAP in 1990, the First American Prevention Center proposed to increase both individual and communal empowerment in several Ojibwe communities. This article reviews the process which occurred in the first of these communities in which the interventions were implemented, and examines quantitative and qualitative results which characterize the population and describe changes associated with the intervention.

## BACKGROUND

The grantee organization, the First American Prevention Center, is located within the primary community and is a tribally chartered organization of the Red Cliff Band of Lake Superior Chippewa. Founded in 1984, the Center's mission is to "translate indigenous teachings into contemporary lifelong learning experiences." The Center is staffed entirely by Native People who have made a long term commitment to prevention and who, collectively, have decades of experience in this field. The Center grew from a grassroots collaboration. In 1981, a group of Ojibwe people in recovery met to discuss the needs of the young people. This group discussed their own, sometimes troubled journeys in coping with living in two cultures and their personal battles with alcohol and drugs. It was agreed that personal successes had been due both to early grounding in values of their native culture and a return in adulthood to these spiritual roots. As a result of these meetings, the group collaborated with several of its members with graduate level education, to develop a curriculum for 4th through 6th graders who were deemed to be at a critical stage of risk. Additional curricula were subsequently produced, the second for kindergarten through 3rd grade, and a third for high school (Red Cliff Wellness Curriculum, 1984).

These "Wellness" curricula provided substance abuse prevention education. The medium or focus of the curricula were on teaching traditional values and skills related to empowerment: problem-solving, decision-making and taking control over circumstances, balanced by spiritual themes of transformation and openness to the Spirit at one's central core. These curricula, funded by Title 5 funds from the Department of Education, were disseminated to other school systems, and are currently being used in 130 schools in Native American communities.

In 1990, the Center was awarded a five year High Risk Youth Demonstration Project through the Center for Substance Abuse Prevention. This project, the Parent, School and Community Partnership Program was designed to reduce the prevalence of tobacco, alcohol, marijuana, and inhalant use among Native American youth residing on or near three rural Indian reservations in the Great Lakes region. Youth in these regions were recognized as being at high risk for development of drug and alcohol problems based on presence of a number of factors. A statewide examination of minority health in Wisconsin (Wisconsin Department of Health and Social Services, 1993) revealed that the poverty rate among Indians in Wisconsin increased 12 percent in the past decade, and Indians were more than three times as likely as other Wisconsin residents to be poor. Thirty-nine percent of the Indian population in Wisconsin is under 18 years of age, and 55 percent of Indian children live in poverty. Wisconsin Indian youth report high levels of substance use and are more likely to report use of tobacco than youth of other ethnic backgrounds.

The Interventions included the school-based cultural curriculum, training of teachers, and two recently developed components, the development of a leadership core group, and a community curriculum.

*The Red Cliff Wellness School Curriculum.* This K-12 school-based substance abuse curriculum was designed to be implemented by trained classroom teachers. The curriculum is culturally-based, incorporating tribal legends and cooperative learning techniques. The goal is to increase school bonding by creating a more nurturing classroom environment, both culturally and personally. The curriculum for each grade includes 20 to 30 separate lessons/activities which address resiliency factors in the individual, peer, and school domains. The curriculum seeks to change individual attitudes and behaviors through a cooperative leaning approach in the school classroom. The curriculum is designed to develop the following resiliency factors in the participants: (a) positive attitudes toward school; (b) positive academic performance; (c) positive attitudes toward tribal identity and values; (d) active participation in cultural activities; (e) personal disapproval of substance use; and (f) perception of risk associated with substance use. This curriculum was provided to the schools involved at no cost. Comparison schools were compensated by receiving the curriculum after they had participated as comparisons. This component was the most developed and articulated element of the intervention, and most amenable to rigorous scientific outcome testing. Measures of substance use in students were obtained at baseline and follow-up in participating and comparison schools.

*Teacher Training.* Key to implementation of the curriculum was the training of teachers. Classroom teachers were trained to implement the curriculum and technical assistance was provided to the teachers and school staff by project staff. Each classroom teacher was required to attend 24 hours of training prior to implementing the curriculum and each school also received 10-20 hours of on-site technical assistance from the Center staff each year. The focus of the training and technical assistance is on developing the knowledge and skills necessary to effectively implement the K-12 curriculum. The training uses a hands-on approach in which teachers are directly involved with using the materials and developing plans for adapting them to the classroom. Through this vehicle, however, the project staff did more than train teachers to deliver curriculum. The training educated and sensitized teachers who often knew little about the culture of their pupils, and increased teachers' knowledge and skills related to substance abuse education.

*Training of Leaders.* A core group of 5-7 community trainers was developed to assume a leadership role in promoting community health.

Volunteers were identified and approached within the community. The core group members were selected based on their willingness and ability to assume a leadership role in promoting community health. The core group members played a key role in planning and conducting all subsequent community training activities. The members of the core group received 32 hours of training designed to prepare them to facilitate training at the community level.

*The Community Curriculum.* This component contained 4 modules:

1. The "Spiritual and Cultural Perspective on Substance Abuse" Module deals with spiritual issues which the developers saw as key to personal and communal recovery. Spirituality and a connection to the spiritual world has historically been important to the Ojibwe both on the individual and communal level. The importance of this factor can be seen in the historical migration of the Ojibwe. As the Ojibwe migrated from Canada to settle around the Great Lakes region, groups settled in areas indicated by the dreams of their members. The gradual loss or distortion of this spirituality was seen by the designers of the module as key to the disintegration of their communities; reawakening this force on the individual and communal level was seen as central to restoration. The module led community groups through a process designed to deal with the tension both on the internal individual level and the communal level related to the conflict between Christianity and traditional religion, which had resulted in internalized oppression, self-doubt and loss of vision and direction. The module also examined the impact of substance abuse on the spiritual and cultural health of Indian communities.

2. "A Family Perspective on Substance Abuse" dealt with the family dynamics of substance abuse. This model was designed to help individuals in the group to conduct a critical analysis of the dynamics of their families. The group examined traditional and other models of marital and family interaction for insight and alternatives to their current situations.

3. "Accessing Resources Through Effective Cooperation Between Tribal and Non-Tribal Agencies" involved the group in organizing for community change. This module works through accessing additional resources and utilizing current resources more effectively. At this stage, the group becomes more aware of possibilities for change on the economic, legal and social levels.

4. "Comprehensive Community-Based Planning" took the community members through a systematic approach to planning to make their vision a reality. The Core Group implemented the Red Cliff Community Training Curriculum with parents, extended family, and community members in open community sessions. Each module took two days (14 hours) to

implement. The broad purpose of the community training is to build the skill and confidence of local community members to create an environment where parents, grandparents, and other community members develop a sense of ownership of community problems and become advocates and activists for change at all levels of the social system. Through the training, community problems and solutions are identified, defined, and described by the community members and solutions developed. All modules were presented to the community. At the request of the community, the Spiritual Module segment was repeated.

## METHODOLOGY AND IMPLEMENTATION

*School Component.* This component was designed to be evaluated with some rigor. Implementation of components was monitored using short forms filled out by teachers after every session. The study design used pre- and posttest measures of participating schools and compared them with a school in another community which agreed to be used as a comparison group in return for receiving the modules at a later date. Students were tested using an anonymous, self-report instrument, the First American Prevention Center Student Survey which incorporated items from Monitoring the Future, the National Household Survey, the Primary Prevention and Awareness, Attitudes, and Usage Scales (Swisher, 1988) and an acculturation scale developed by the National Center for American Indian and Alaska Native Mental Health. Outcome variables included: substance use, attitudes toward substance use and perceptions of harmfulness, attitudes toward school, academic achievement, absenteeism, and cultural involvement. The high risk youth surveyed included all students in grades 4-12 at eight rural schools serving Indian reservations in northern Wisconsin and Minnesota. Surveys were administered on a yearly basis to students in their classrooms over a period of three years.

The instrument evolved over the course of the project, increasing in scope and complexity each year. The survey designed by the original evaluation contractors for use in Year One did not systematically address substance use or academic success, and did not include any measures of cultural involvement. Revisions to the survey for use in year two improved the substance use and academic success measures to a limited extent. These difficulties were largely a result of the fact that the evaluation contractors initially involved with the project lacked specific experience in evaluating prevention programs and did not demonstrate the cultural competence necessary to work with the targeted communities. After two years, a project staff member was assigned to work full-time on the evaluation and the project contracted with a new team of more experienced evaluators, and a final revision took place prior to year three. In addition to improving the quality of the evaluation, these changes also resulted in the development of a more positive staff attitude toward the evaluation. The development of a more team-oriented effort increased the perceived value of the evaluation and encouraged a sense of staff ownership.

However, these modifications to the Student Survey also created difficulties for the project. Not only did the yearly revisions of the instrument consume valuable staff time and program resources, it also restricted the outcome evaluation of the classroom component. While the modifications to the survey resulted in an increase in the quality and quantity of data, the amount of consistently gathered information across the three years decreased. The limited number of overlapping items across the three years of data collection somewhat constrained the analyses which could be conducted. These survey data were examined to characterize the population in terms of use and relationships between use and other characteristics as well as to compare the intervention group with the comparison group.

As this element of the intervention was implemented and data collected in several communities, data from these additional implementation sites was included in the analysis. A total of 1,937 surveys were completed over the three-year data collection period. There were 755 surveys received in Year One, 620 in Year Two, and 562 in Year Three from eight schools in five communities in Wisconsin and Minnesota. Respondents were 50% male, 50% female; 38% (736) were 4th and 5th grade students, 36% (697) in grades six through eight, and 26% (504) were high school students. Seventy-four percent of the students were Indian. Sixty-one percent of the students reported living in two-parent households, 26% lived with their mother only, five percent with father only, and eight percent with other adults.

A subset of this population was used for comparison of treatment and comparison groups. Data points for collection were the beginning of year one prior to the implementation of the curriculum, the second data point was at the end of the year of implementation, and the third data collection was done at the end of the second year after implementation. Classrooms of fourth, fifth and sixth grade students (in fifth, sixth and seventh grade at final test point) were tested at a participating location and at a comparison location which had agreed to collect data during years one and two in exchange for receiving the curriculum in year three. Number of subjects at time point one was 82 participants and 169 comparisons, at point two: 75 and 162, and at point three: 80 and 76 respectively. Two-way analysis of variance (ANOVA) was used to compare the level of substance use in the two sites.

*Training of Classroom Teachers.* While the application defined this element as an intervention in its own right, the evaluation design implemented treated this element as a process variable. Measures with teachers focused on implementation of the curriculum, and did not measure impact on attitudes of teachers toward their students. The process information gathered, however, provided valuable information with regard to improving and measuring implementation. There was a broad range among teachers in how the curriculum was used. While some teachers used the curriculum extensively, others used it only in a perfunctory manner or only infrequently chose to include it in their classroom activities. As these discrepancies surfaced, project staff found themselves modifying measures to more clearly and accurately measure implementation in ways which would encourage teacher cooperation. Project staff found repeated training sessions were required due to the frequent staff turnovers, which often plague school systems serving Native American youth. Given limitations of implementation, the significant impact of the curriculum upon outcome measures in spite of these barriers is even more impressive.

*Core Group Formation.* Core community members were carefully selected to include individuals who were respected by the community. This group named themselves "Soft Winds" and as a group began to carry out leadership functions in the community. Some members of the core group, initially hesitant to lead community trainings, not only showed ease in such roles, but eventually traveled to other communities to provide trainings. While this element of the intervention was considered by the evaluation team to be only a vehicle for curriculum administration, the activities of this group and the future impact of their formation upon the community are being followed. Case study comparison of the composition of this group and their successful dynamics with other programs which may experience less successful leadership formation, may offer information of value to the fledgling study of community systems and change.

*Red Cliff Community Training Curriculum.* The first module, on Spirituality, was offered first. Thirty-five community members attended this training, a powerful experience which brought tears, reconciliation and a heightened sense of community. Many people reported experiencing a transformation and healing through this workshop. Attendance climbed steadily as the modules progressed; by the fifth training session, a requested repeat of the first Spirituality module, 200 community members attended.

## RESULTS

### Student Survey

*Characterization of the Population.* Analyses examined substance use, school bonding and relationship between cultural affiliation and substance use. Examination of usage rates for the target population showed levels of use by students aged 12-17 to be higher than the national average reported in the 1993 National Household Survey (NHS) by the National Institute on Drug Abuse (NIDA, 1994). Thirty day alcohol use was somewhat higher (29%) than that reported in the NHS (18.0%), however, marijuana use (22% vs. 4.9% in the NHS) and cigarette use (42% vs. 9.6% in the NHS) were considerably higher than the national average. Measures of 30 day use in the baseline year showed a steady, almost identical increase across the age groups for alcohol, cigarettes and marijuana (see Figure 1); inhalant use flattened out in middle school. A comparison of Indian students with non-Indian students in the schools showed that Indians were less likely to report that they enjoyed school (21% of Indians vs. 39% of non-Indians, p = .002), less likely to like their school subjects (16% vs. 29%, p = .02) and less likely to report being "A" students (14% vs. 40%, p = .04).

Table 1 shows the relationship between substance use and cultural involvement practices. For the group including males and females, attendance at cultural events was positively correlated with marijuana and cigarette use; for males but not for females, participation was also correlated with alcohol use. Participation in tribal ceremonies was weakly correlated with cigarette use for the group, but more strongly correlated among males with marijuana use. There was a discrepancy between males and females in the relationship between substance abuse and the perceived importance of Indian identity; males rating the importance of Indian identity highly were more likely to use marijuana, while females rating it highly were less likely to use alcohol than their counterparts.

*Outcome Comparisons.* Figure 2 shows reported use of alcohol, marijuana and cigarettes in the past 30 days. Analysis of past month alcohol use revealed a significant 2-way interaction of site and time (F = 4.0, df = 2, p < .01). The intervention appeared to have some effect in slowing, in participants, the rise in alcohol use shown in the comparison group. Past month marijuana use revealed a significant main effect of site (F = 15.6, df = 1, p < .001). While marijuana use at both sites remained relatively low at followup, comparison site students reported higher levels of use than project site students at all three data collection points. Cigarette smoking, which was not targeted by the intervention increased over time at both sites.

Reported likelihood of use of alcohol or marijuana if asked by friends

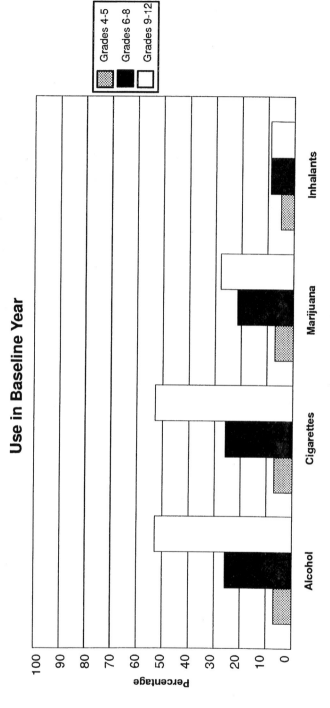

FIGURE 1. Substance Use in Baseline Year for Grades 4-5, 6-8 and 9-12

**Use in Baseline Year**

TABLE 1. Correlations Between Cultural Involvement Measures and Past Month Use of Substances for Indian High School Students (Grades 9-12)

| | Past Month Alcohol Use | Past Month Marijuana Use | Past Month Cigarette Use |
|---|---|---|---|
| **Overall** | | | |
| Importance of Indian identity | −.05 | .08 | −.00 |
| Attendance at cultural events | .20 | .24** | .34** |
| Participation in tribal ceremonies | .03 | .21** | .20* |
| **Males** | | | |
| Importance of Indian identity | .11 | .25* | −.08 |
| Attendance at cultural events | .28* | .22 | .28* |
| Participation in tribal ceremonies | .15 | .31** | .16 |
| **Females** | | | |
| Importance of Indian identity | −.38** | −.20 | .09 |
| Attendance at cultural events | .14 | .30* | .38** |
| Participation in tribal ceremonies | −.13 | .06 | .24 |

\* $p < .05$
\*\* $p < .01$

FIGURE 2. Substance Use at Project Site and Comparison Site

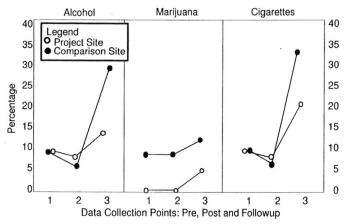

was also investigated. Baseline likelihood of accepting alcohol and marijuana was not significantly different at the two sites. ANOVA on alcohol use revealed a significant main effect of time ($F = 41.45$, $df = 2$, $p < .001$). Students in both schools were more likely to accept alcohol from their friends as they grew older, there was no significant difference between the two sites at the third time point. ANOVA on marijuana use revealed a significant interaction of site and time ($F = 4.85$, $df = 2$, $p < .01$). Project site students were less likely to accept marijuana at the final data point than comparison students. Figure 3 shows reported likelihood of substance use for the two groups if offered alcohol or marijuana.

### Qualitative Results

A number of changes were observed in the community:

- There was evidence of increased social bonding. A waning tradition of "visiting" was recaptured.
- A number of families involved in the training who previously either had not recognized or were afraid to admit to family problems took action to get help for their problems.
- A key concern identified by the community was their strained relationship with the school system. Activities began to focus upon changing the relationship between the community and this system. (1) Children receiving the Wellness Curriculum in the project's school component were emboldened in 1992 to stage a walkout from their school. (2) A group of community members met with the school board and provided recommendations to deal with problems identified by the students. This group requested and received support for a study which was done to assess different learning styles and ways to accommodate the diversity of styles. (3) The community organized an inservice training for teachers in which elders told teachers about their grandchildren, passed on stories, explained concerns, discussed their views on appropriate discipline, and exchanged questions and answers. (4) Teachers were invited to a dinner in their honor, at which the elders formally entrusted them with the care of their grandchildren.
- Political action evolved. (1) After seeking counsel and investigating the situation, two local women elders organized a protest at the local establishment where it was believed that drugs were sold. (2) In the final year of the project, youth participants carried out, under their own initiative, a dramatic ceremony on the steps of the State Capital in which they symbolically returned and poured out liquor

representing their personal rejection of alcohol use and their political objection to the use of alcohol as a negotiating tool in the historical treaty making process.

## *DISCUSSION*

This project represents a potential wealth of information regarding community empowerment. This took place at several levels. The process in this community was gradual and succeeded both in achieving community cohesion and in avoiding destructive internal confrontation. Much of this success can be attributed to the philosophical approach of the staff. The emphasis of the model was developmental, nurturing a gradual growth of personal and communal strength. Attention to details as minute as arranging the seating at training sessions to minimize conflict was helpful. Intimate insider knowledge of relationships and informal power structures in the community was utilized to avoid derailment of the process. Actions developed by the community as a result of this process display creative and effective ways of bringing things into harmony, rather

FIGURE 3. Likelihood of Substance Use at Project Site and Comparison Site

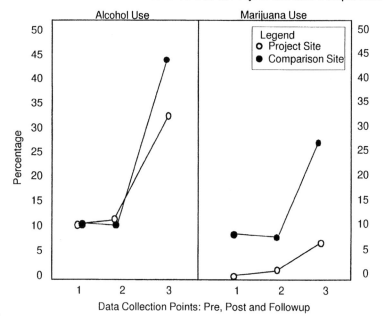

than adding to disharmony by being confrontational and reactionary. A second level involved the relationship between the school and the community which was renegotiated in a creative manner. A third level was the evaluation which the project needed to carry out to satisfy funding requirements. During the course of the grant, there was an evolution in the orientation toward evaluation: from a suspicion of evaluation to active collaboration in the process, from use of imposed standardized instruments poorly matched for the population and outcomes, to actively selecting and refining instruments; from dependence upon an aloof outside expert to one chosen as an appropriate collaborator. In all these areas, the project appears to have negotiated successfully what Labonte refers to as a dance: "Empowerment is not static. It is a fascinating dynamic of power given and taken all at once, a dialectical dance between consensus and conflict, professional expertise and lay wisdom, hierarchic institutions and community circles" (Bernstein et al., 1994, p. 285).

While this model evolved at the grassroots level, it shows significant parallels to the Freirian model. It takes a long-term view in focusing a structured K-12 curriculum on youth, which is designed to improve self concept and to teach problem-solving, decision-making and taking control over circumstances to the upcoming generation. This curriculum as well as the community curriculum are oriented by traditional spiritual themes. As the school curriculum does on the individual level, the community curriculum appears to strengthen the social network of the community, and provides tools for analysis of the individual's personal, family and communal spheres and their relationship to structures of mainstream society. The youth and the larger community have both successfully organized and carried out action to change their environments.

Much can be learned from these preliminary results. One lesson is that change toward increased empowerment can be successful using strengths in Native American communities. This change, however, takes time and can not be forced without disempowering individuals and communities. As originally designed, the project was overly ambitious, aiming, on a very limited budget, to complete the process in 15 sites. At the end of the five year project, after several revisions to timetables, the process was fully implemented in this one site and in various stages of progress in four other sites.

Despite the limitations of the quantitative components of the evaluation due to restructuring over time, valuable information was generated both with regard to description of the population, and in terms of outcome comparisons. The evaluation profiled the population, using cross-sectional sampling to document the increase in substance use across age groups, tripling between elementary school and high school. Thirty day alcohol use among high school students was somewhat higher than the national average, however, both marijuana and cigarette use were about four times the national average. Indian students were also seen to be encountering difficulties in the school environment; compared with non-Indian students in their schools, Indian students were less likely to enjoy school, to like their subjects, and to be "A" students. Cultural affiliation which is generally perceived as a protective factor was revealed as an area that needs more careful and focused study. The results from this project indicated that increased frequency of attendance at pow-wows was associated with increased use of substances. Also, the relationship between Indian identity and substance use differed for males and females, identity being associated with decreased use in females, but increased use in males. We view these findings as preliminary at best since they are based on very limited assessment techniques, only three items were included on our questionnaire to measure cultural affiliation. More comprehensive methods for assessing cultural affiliation need to be developed and employed before conclusions can be drawn about this complex area of human behavior.

The outcome evaluation of the curriculum revealed that student substance use and expectation of use was impacted. Fewer students who received the curriculum reported use of alcohol in the past month than students in the comparison group. The expectation to use marijuana was also lower at the project site than at the comparison site, although this was possibly a function of the lower initial rate of use in the two sites.

It is difficult to evaluate programs such as these. As Wallerstein and Sanchez-Merki have noted: "Research into Freirian programs poses special difficulties, because many of the objectives of change are not preset. Participants in Freirian interventions often choose their own change targets as they become engaged in the process. Community-level change requires long-term commitment, with both intended and unintended results" (1994, p. 110). The fact that the science of community change is still in some ways in its infancy, does not preclude scientific work. Case studies such as the current one, if properly documented, can provide the beginnings of a database which will allow commonalties to surface, phases to be identified and instruments to be used to measure achievement of these phases.

Because systems are interrelated, field studies do not allow for teasing apart effects of causal factors. For example, two of the four interventions began as focused on the school system. Groups formed by the other interventions also later chose to focus on changing the relationship between the community and the school system. Outcome data on substance use of youth reported and subsequent activism of youth can not be attributed to any single one of these interventions. Future studies of community change need extensive documentation, and thick ethnographic level description to allow post-hoc analysis and generation of hypotheses with regard to key elements in successful programs.

One such element in need of documentation is the personal element involved in administering curriculum. Measures such as extent of use of the material, changes in teacher attitude toward the population, teacher knowledge of and involvement with their students' culture, and possibly some measure of teacher bonding, such as teacher retention, decreased teacher burnout, and attitudes of parents toward teachers may be needed to test curriculum components as an intervention affecting the system in its own right.

## REFERENCES

Bernstein, E., Wallerstein, N., Braithwaite, R., Gutierrez, L., Labonte, R., Zimmerman, M. (1994). Empowerment forum: a dialogue between guest editorial board members. Health Education Quarterly, 21, 281-294.

Freire, P. (1970). Pedagogy of the Oppressed. Seabury Press, New York.

Minority health in Wisconsin. (1993) Wisconsin Department of Health and Social Services: Madison, WI.

Red Cliff Wellness Curriculum. (1984). Bayfield, WI: First American Prevention Center. Substance Abuse and Mental Health Services Administration. (1994) National Household Survey on Drug Abuse: Population Estimates 1993. SAMHSA, DHHS Publication #(SMA) 94-3017.

Swisher, J.D. (1988) Primary Prevention and awareness, attitudes, and usage scales. State College: PA.

Wallerstein, N. (1992). Powerlessness, empowerment, and health: implications for health promotion programs. American J. of Health Promotion, 6, 197-205.

Wallerstein, N. and Sanchez-Merki, V. (1994). Freirian praxis in health education: research results from an adolescent prevention program. Health Education Research, 9, 105-118.

# Index

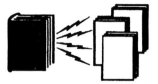

# Haworth
# DOCUMENT DELIVERY
## SERVICE

This valuable service provides a single-article order form for any article from a Haworth journal.

- *Time Saving:* No running around from library to library to find a specific article.
- *Cost Effective:* All costs are kept down to a minimum.
- *Fast Delivery:* Choose from several options, including same-day FAX.
- *No Copyright Hassles:* You will be supplied by the original publisher.
- *Easy Payment:* Choose from several easy payment methods.

---

*Open Accounts Welcome for . . .*
- Library Interlibrary Loan Departments
- Library Network/Consortia Wishing to Provide Single-Article Services
- Indexing/Abstracting Services with Single Article Provision Services
- Document Provision Brokers and Freelance Information Service Providers

---

### MAIL or *FAX* THIS ENTIRE ORDER FORM TO:

Haworth Document Delivery Service
The Haworth Press, Inc.
10 Alice Street
Binghamton, NY 13904-1580

**or FAX:** 1-800-895-0582
**or CALL:** 1-800-342-9678
9am-5pm EST

---

PLEASE SEND ME PHOTOCOPIES OF THE FOLLOWING SINGLE ARTICLES:

1) Journal Title: _____
   Vol/Issue/Year:_____Starting & Ending Pages:_____
Article Title:_____

2) Journal Title: _____
   Vol/Issue/Year:_____Starting & Ending Pages:_____
Article Title:_____

3) Journal Title: _____
   Vol/Issue/Year:_____Starting & Ending Pages:_____
Article Title:_____

4) Journal Title: _____
   Vol/Issue/Year:_____Starting & Ending Pages:_____
Article Title:_____

---

**(See other side for Costs and Payment Information)**

*COSTS:* Please figure your cost to order quality copies of an article.

1. Set-up charge per article: $8.00
   ($8.00 × number of separate articles) _____

2. Photocopying charge for each article:

   1-10 pages: $1.00 _____

   11-19 pages: $3.00 _____

   20-29 pages: $5.00 _____

   30+ pages: $2.00/10 pages _____

3. Flexicover (optional): $2.00/article _____

4. Postage & Handling: US: $1.00 for the first article/
   $.50 each additional article _____

   Federal Express: $25.00 _____

   Outside US: $2.00 for first article/
   $.50 each additional article_____

5. Same-day FAX service: $.35 per page _____

## GRAND TOTAL: _____

*METHOD OF PAYMENT:* (please check one)

❑ Check enclosed     ❑ Please ship and bill. PO # _____
(sorry we can ship and bill to bookstores only! All others must pre-pay)

❑ Charge to my credit card:  ❑ Visa;   ❑ MasterCard;   ❑ Discover;
                             ❑ American Express;

Account Number:_____ Expiration date:_____

Signature: X_____

Name: _____ Institution: _____

Address: _____

_____

City: _____ State:_____ Zip:_____

Phone Number: _____ FAX Number: _____

## MAIL or *FAX* THIS ENTIRE ORDER FORM TO:

| | |
|---|---|
| Haworth Document Delivery Service | **or FAX:** 1-800-895-0582 |
| The Haworth Press, Inc. | **or CALL:** 1-800-342-9678 |
| 10 Alice Street | 9am-5pm EST) |
| Binghamton, NY 13904-1580 | |